Battleground Europe

The Western Dunkirk Corridor 1940

Battleground Europe

The Western Dunkirk Corridor 1940

Ledringhem, Wormhout, Bambecque and West-Cappel

Jerry Murland

Series Editor
Nigel Cave

Pen & Sword
MILITARY

First published in Great Britain in 2022 by
PEN & SWORD MILITARY
an imprint of Pen & Sword Books Ltd
Yorkshire – Philadelphia

ISBN 978-1-52674-318-3

A CIP catalogue record for this book is available from the British Library.

Typeset by Concept, Huddersfield, West Yorkshire, HD4 5JL.
Printed and bound in England by CPI Group (UK) Ltd, Croydon CR0 4YY.

MIX
Paper | Supporting responsible forestry
FSC® C013604
FSC
www.fsc.org

Pen & Sword Books Ltd incorporates the imprints of Aviation, Atlas, Family History, Fiction, Maritime, Military, Discovery, Politics, History, Archaeology, Select, Wharncliffe Local History, Wharncliffe True Crime, Military Classics, Wharncliffe Transport, Leo Cooper, The Praetorian Press, Remember When, White Owl, Seaforth Publishing and Frontline Books.

For a complete list of Pen & Sword titles please contact
PEN & SWORD BOOKS LTD
47 Church Street, Barnsley, South Yorkshire, S70 2AS, England
E-mail: enquiries@pen-and-sword.co.uk
Website: www.pen-and-sword.co.uk
or
PEN & SWORD BOOKS
1950 Lawrence Rd, Havertown, PA 19083, USA
E-mail: uspen-and-sword@casematepublishers.com
Website: www.penandswordbooks.com

Contents

List of Maps

Introduction by the Series Editor

With this book, *The Western Dunkirk Corridor*, Jerry Murland completes his survey of the major part of the BEF's campaign in France and Flanders 1940 that culminated in its evacuation from the beaches of the Channel, largely just to the east of Dunkirk (or, more accurately, Dunkerque). He has done this in a total of seven volumes and has provided us with a comprehensive account and guide to this very brief – and disastrous to both British and French arms – German offensive that was, effectively, all over within four weeks of its launch. The French fought on, as did several British formations and units; indeed, attempts were made to reinforce them. The fate of those members of the BEF at St Valery, notably many from the 51st (Highland) Division, will be covered in Jerry's final volume in the *Battleground* series on the 1940 campaign.

The cataclysmic German onslaught was an absolute disaster, as Churchill readily recognised. On the bright side, Operation Dynamo (ie the evacuation centred on the Dunkirk beaches, 26 May to 4 June); Operation Cycle (10 to 13 June), which evacuated allied troops from the Le Havre area; and Operation Aerial (15 to 25 June, although unofficially and in reality it continued until well into August), which evacuated men where it could from France's Mediterranean and Atlantic ports, did manage to bring to British shores the vast majority of the British troops deployed to the continent. Of about 400,000 men, however, some 65,000 were casualties: about 25,000 killed or wounded and the remainder captured. In addition there were the other allied troops who made it to Britain, mainly French, getting on for 200,000 of them.

On the much longer, negative side of the balance sheet, the BEF had lost vast, truly immense, amounts of equipment: the British were left with the makings of an army but one that was almost bereft of the weapons of war. And, of course, it had lost – or was soon to lose – its last major (indeed only remaining) ally on the continent, when an armistice between Germany and what was to become the new Vichy regime in France, went into effect in the very early hours of 25 June. Britain was reduced to depending on the Royal Navy to safeguard it from an invasion and, in due course, the RAF to defend it from the air.

The British, however, used the nation's peculiar genius to turn disaster into something that seemed as though it might be some sort of victory by turning the evacuation from the beaches into a heroic and ultimately successful national endeavour that served to boost the nation's morale. Whatever the myth surrounding Operation Dynamo might be, the effects of the skilfully massaged propaganda (although one cannot for a moment deny the bravery of all of those involved in Dynamo's execution, civilians as well as servicemen) seem to have succeeded in its purpose. The nation was not beaten into submission and it is probably accurate to say that a renewed national sense of purpose was one of the clearest, if intangible, benefits of the largely successful evacuations.

One of the problems of the narrative of the events of May and early June is that much popular attention has been focussed on the evacuation of the BEF. What has often been lost to historians and those with an interest in the campaign, apart from the twin memories of a stunningly successful German *blitzkrieg* invasion and the makeshift evacuations, is the conduct of the short campaign that was fought to counter the attack. In a rather crude shorthand, this came down to, originally, a counter-offensive plan, which then fell back to an attempt to form defensive lines and ultimately the decision was made to evacuate the vast bulk of the BEF and French troops as necessary from the beaches around Dunkirk.

This means that the desperate battles fought to hold the line initially and then to hold the German advance back or at least delay it when the evacuation was ordered and the perimeter established are little known. There is a natural tendency to see this as the Germans sweeping in from the east, but in fact it was a pincer movement, with the Germans closing in on all sides except from the north.

This 'pincer movement' became all too apparent to me when I was writing the prototype Battleground book, the large format *Battleground Europe*, which was published in 1990. Until I started writing that book I was all but unaware of the determined defence of Calais (and, to a lesser extent, Boulogne), a defence that last three days between 24 and the early hours of 27 May and which played an important, possibly crucial, part in the broadly successful evacuation to the east over subsequent days. Indeed, there were evacuations of a significant number of troops from the docks of both Boulogne and Calais.

Away from the beaches there was often intensive fighting and much 'making-do' of fighting forces, combining units into temporary 'Forces', as lines were held and, ultimately, outer defensive perimeters for the Dunkirk evacuation held and only grudgingly given up in the face of overwhelming force. The *Western Dunkirk Corridor* covers fighting to the south of Dunkirk. The landscape of the area is flat, very flat and the local settlements are not particularly architecturally distinguished, with the notable exception of Esquelbecq; here a much-restored chateau and impressive church – both having suffered from the ravages of the French Revolution along with other more mundane events, such as fires – dominate a pleasant market place. Wormhout was a town of some 3,000 people in 1939 and Esquelbecq about half that number.

The fighting involved the usual mixture of regular and territorial units, infantry, artillery and some yeomanry. Vehicles – or at least functioning vehicles – were becoming something of a luxury by this stage in the retreat. Defences had to be prepared rapidly and with no adequate idea of where the main threat was likely to emerge as the area held outside the evacuation perimeter continued to shrink under the German pressure. This is an account of troops 'making do', with commanders trying their utmost to restrain the advancing enemy whilst the evacuations proceeded as rapidly as possible to the north. It seems to me that because of the relatively small size of the British forces involved it becomes easier to feel closer to the actions than if this had involved a narrative based on traditional, large formations.

By and large the British defenders were soldiers who had already endured much in the few weeks preceding the actions described here, had been driven from pillar to post for days, had endured privations and discomfort and, of course, the morale sapping reality of going backwards and of facing a very uncertain future. Practically no one had a full understanding of the 'big' picture but all could appreciate that, whatever it might be, it certainly was not a pretty thing.

Wormhout and Esquelbecq are amongst the few place names in this area of France, close to the Belgian border, that have a special resonance amongst those who take a deeper interest in the events of 1940 than the average Briton. For it was here that an infamous massacre took place in a ramshackle barn in a field that lay between the two places, and where eighty or more soldiers, principally from the Royal Warwickshire Regiment, were murdered by soldiers of the SS.

An account of that massacre was also included in that first Battleground book. My awareness of it was aroused by an article in the *Times* in about 1989 but I had also heard of it from the proprietor of a campsite I often used at Boiry Notre Dame, near Arras. In the course of conversation Esquelbecq came up and he told me that he was born and raised near there and was present in 1940; how he and his father cut branches to camouflage French guns and of the harrowing things that he witnessed. Two French women were beaten to death in a barn; he saw members of the Cheshire Regiment being bayoneted, beaten and shot: he buried three of these Cheshires himself. This ghastliness mirrored that at Le Paradis (which is described in *The Canal Line* in this series). In both cases the massacres were deliberately ordered and staged, with a large group of men who had been taken prisoner deliberately moved to a place of execution. In both cases it was members of the SS who were responsible. It also seems very likely that those in the barn were not the only ones murdered; others, the evidence indicates, were casually executed by a roadside.

It is quite certain that in the Great War there were many cases of men who had surrendered who were shot or otherwise killed without much qualm, no matter how much they might have tried to surrender. Apart from a number of atrocities against civilians in the early months of that war, however, these tended to be isolated incidents – a reaction of men, for example, who had seen comrades and friends killed by, say, machine gun bullets and who were overcome by fury or vengeance when the machine gunner sought to surrender when he or his gun team were left with no alternative. These incidents were in the heat of battle and there is little indication on the Western Front that there was anything like this level of deliberate, effectively organised, execution of prisoners who had surrendered and whose surrender had been accepted. It was shocking, so much so that there was a disinclination to believe in many circles that such atrocities were much more than over-exaggerated propaganda. Of course, there were far more examples of this kind of inhuman brutality to come; there had perhaps been some indications during the Polish campaign in 1939 but the ferocity of the fighting in the Eastern Front took this barbarity to a whole new level of awfulness.

In recent years much has been done locally to retain the memory of the massacre in that barn; a tranquil area of remembrance and the restored building provides a suitable place in which to contemplate man's capacity for brutality but also of the powers of courage, comradeship and obligation to others.

As a side note, whilst engaging in some work near le Quesnel in about 2015, on the right flank of the Canadian Corps' advance in August 1918, I decided to go off the beaten track to visit a small, isolated CWGC cemetery, Manitoba Cemetery. Whilst driving along the single-track road I noticed on my left a small monument. It commemorates thirty-one Breton soldiers who were executed – put in front of two machine guns by the Germans (thought to be SS) on 7 June – in the fields behind it. There were a few who survived, all wounded to a greater degree or the other and only a couple who lived to tell the tale. The casualties were left to rot in the fields for over six weeks. Elsewhere a particular target of the Germans were soldiers from the French African colonies, particularly the Senegalese and, occasionally, their white officers. The most notable case was at Chasselay, in the Lyonnais; but some fifty men of the 24e Régiment de Tirailleurs Sénégalais were reportedly executed at Aubigny (Somme) on 24 May 1940. In all, one estimate has 3,000 Senegalese soldiers as being 'executed' (which seems to me to not call it as it was, that is cold blooded murder), so far as I know, by elements of the SS, in May and June 1940. In their case their 'crime' was to be black, worthless and, indeed, sub-human – all anathema to the poisonous ideology that was spouted by Hitler and his devotees.

The final actions in front of the evacuation perimeter have very much the feel of the 'forlorn hope' about them. And yet … Every day the Germans were held up, every time their advance was disrupted and manpower had to be deployed and then, eventually, brought back and reorganised, every disruption brought time for the desperate efforts to embark as many of the BEF as was possible. The largely unsung heroism of these men, many of

The inscription on the memorial reads: 'At this point, on 7 June 1940, 31 disarmed French soldiers of the 41e RI and 10e RAD from Rennes were massacred by the Nazis.' The plaque below commemorates Lieutenant Colonel Loichot of the 41st, who died of typhus on 25 May 1945, shortly after his liberation from Dachau, where he had been interned for being involved in the resistance.

whom made the ultimate sacrifice, and who provided extra days and hours that allowed Dynamo to proceed for as long as it did, deserve much wider appreciation; Jerry Murland's series of books provides us with the narrative and the guidance to be able to follow in their footsteps.

Nigel Cave
Ratcliffe College

Author's Introduction

The story of 144 Brigade's defence of Wormhout and Bambecque must rank in importance alongside the defence of Cassel and Hazebrouck by 145 Brigade; however, what is often forgotten in the uncertainty that surrounded Wormhout and Bambecque is the heroic defence of West-Cappel and Vyfweg (les Cinq Chemins today) by the Welsh Guards and the 1/Fife and Forfar Yeomanry (1/F&F Yeomanry). Brigadier Norman's composite brigade was the final piece in the jigsaw of defence on the western flank of the Dunkerque Corridor and, after the last stand of the 2/Royal Warwicks and the 8/Worcesters, Norman's brigade held the line south of Bergues, containing the attacking German units at great cost, until the perimeter at Dunkerque had been established. He and the remnants of his brigade left Vyfweg as the Germans were entering from the south. The full story of the evacuation of the BEF from Dunkerque can be read in the Battleground Europe publication: *The Dunkerque Perimeter and Evacuation 1940*.

The defence of Wormhout in 1940 has long been associated with the massacre of British servicemen after they had surrendered and been taken prisoner. The events in the barn at La Plaine au Bois will always be considered to be one of the most appalling acts of the Second World War, carried out by elements of the *Liebstandarte* Regiment, in what looked very much like revenge; a massacre that was almost second nature to this group of fanatical followers of Adolf Hitler. Up against the regular troops of the 2/Warwicks and their supporting units, the *Liebstandarte* found no easy victory at Wormhout in an encounter that saw their regimental commander, *Gruppenführer* Otto 'Sepp' Dietrich, having to take shelter in a roadside ditch away from the fury of the Cheshire machine gunners. Then again, what is often overshadowed by the events in the barn is the series of other murders of civilians and British soldiers that took place as the *Liebstandarte* overwhelmed the fragile defence of the Warwicks. Captain 'Tony' Crook, the Warwicks' Medical Officer, draws attention to just one of these incidents as he was marched into captivity past the bodies of A Company men, who he felt sure had been murdered in cold blood. Another incident involving the Worcesters at Bambecque is related by Lieutenant Roger Cleverley of C Company, who writes in his diary that all the wounded were shot by a commander of the *Liebstandarte*. Apart from hearsay and diary entries, there is little evidence to support the nature of the deaths of these men but, in the opinion of the author, there is no doubt that many British soldiers met their premature end after they had surrendered in the fields and on the pavements of Wormhout and Bambecque.

The sharp eyed amongst you will have noticed that I have used the French spelling of place names throughout, the only exception being where a quote, book title or cemetery has used the anglicized form of 'Dunkirk'.

Ranks and Abbreviations

PSM is an abbreviation of Platoon Sergeant Major, an appointment that was short-lived and carried the rank of warrant officer class III (WOIII), while armoured regiments, such as the 1/F&F Yeomanry, used the rank Troop Sergeant Major (TSM). The ranks were created in 1938, designed to give NCOs experience in commanding units previously commanded by commissioned officers. No promotions to the rank were made after 1940.

The ranks given to each individual are those that were held in May 1940 and do not reflect any subsequent promotion received unless stated. When describing the fighting I have often referred to modern day road numbering in order to give the reader using current maps of the area a more precise location.

When describing units and formations I have used a form of abbreviation: for example, after its first mention in the text, the 2nd Battalion Royal Warwickshire Regiment becomes 2/Warwicks and the 8th Battalion Worcestershire Regiment becomes 8/Worcesters. German army formations and units are a little more complex. Within the infantry regiment there were three battalions – each one approximately the size of a British battalion – and, again, I have abbreviated when describing these units. Thus, the 90th Infantry Regiment becomes IR 90, while the second battalion within that regiment is abbreviated to II/IR 90. Each infantry battalion was broken down into four companies, each of whom was given an Arabic numeral, for example, 3 *Kompanie.*

Below is a comparative table of equivalent ranks that should go some way towards assisting the reader in understanding the correlation between British, Wehrmacht and SS ranks.

British	**SS**	**Wehrmacht**
Private	Schütze	Infanterist
Lance Corporal	Sturmmann	Gefreiter
Corporal	Rottenfürer	Obergefreiter
Sergeant	Scharführer	Unteroffizer
Second Lieutenant	Untersturmführer	Leutnant
Lieutenant	Obersturmführer	Oberleutnant
Captain	Hauptsturmführer	Hauptmann
Major	Sturmbannführer	Major
Lieutenant Colonel	Obersturmbannführer	Oberstleutnant
Colonel	Standartenführer	Oberst
Brigadier	Brigadeführer	–
Major General	Gruppenführer	Generalmajor
Lieutenant General	Obergruppenführer	Generaloberst

Early History

The village of Ledringhem is thought to have been occupied since Gaulish times and the nearby Roman road, now the D52, leading from Cassel to the sea, was very probably the reason for an early settlement on the site. The village is mentioned in 782 under the name Leondringas and again in 1330, where the name Ledringhem appears in a manuscript relating to the Battle of Cassel. In September 1852 two workers discovered a hoard of buried treasure consisting of approximately 35,000 coins, each weighing around 6g, dating back to 250BC. The coins were 45 percent gold, 35 percent silver and 20 percent copper and said to have been the fortune of a Gallic leader.

Wormhout

The town was similarly occupied and is cited in the 7th Century as a settlement that had developed around the Benedictine monastery, destroyed by the Normans in the 9th Century. Wormhout undoubtedly suffered in the numerous wars between France and Spain that constantly damaged the tranquillity of Flanders. Today only a few people in Wormhout still speak Flemish, French speakers forming a majority.

An aerial photograph of modern day Wormhout, showing Place du Général de Gaulle, with the church at the far end. Taken from the north by Fabien Patoor, the building formally occupied by the 2/Royal Warwicks, at the corner of Rue d'Esquelbecq, is shown in the bottom right hand corner and the former brickworks, used as a temporary headquarters by the 5/Gloucesters, is on the left.

The plaque to commemorate members of the BEF on the D55 at Wormhout.

As with many towns in Flanders, Wormhout has its giants, in this case displayed during the carnival on the third Sunday after Mardi Gras; while a thriving weekly market is held every Wednesday morning. Those of you who are in the area in December can take advantage of the Christmas market. Further information about these and other events can be obtained from the Tourist Office in the town square, currently located at 60 Place du Gènèral de Gaulle. There is, apart from the memorial on Plaine au Bois, another on the left of the D55 as you drive out of town. Situated on the Allée Llandudno, the plaque commemorates all British servicemen who served in the area during the Second World War.

Esquelbecq

The village is dominated by the 13th century Château Bergerot, which is accessed by two bridges and is surrounded by a moat. It is assumed that a first wooden structure existed in the 9th Century to protect it from northern invasions, but there is no evidence that it was at the present location. The château and its outbuildings were registered in the French supplementary Historical Monument List in July 1944. In September 1984, the Esquelbecq Heritage Preservation Committee was created, allowing for

An aerial photograph of Château Bergerot and its ornamental gardens at Esquelbecq. The corner of Place Alphonse Bergerot can be seen on the right.

the château's designation as a Historical Monument. Although its interior cannot be visited (it is a private residence), the gardens are currently open to the public from May to mid September, Friday to Sunday, from 2.00pm until 6.00pm. Reservations are required for all guided and self-guided group visits. The Esquelbecq Tourist Office can be found on 9 Place Alphonse Bergerot (email: ot.hautsdeflandre-esquelbecq@laposte.net). The château was occupied by the German army from May 28 1940 until September 5 1944.

The village is also a regional centre for the selling of old and new books through bookshops and regular markets. The book markets are held on the third Sunday of each month in Maison du Westhoek, the same building that houses the Plaine au Bois Museum, which was opened in the village square in 2017 and contains many of the photographs and archives from the collection of Guy Rommelaere, together with a short film of the events of May 1940. Those visiting the massacre site would undoubtedly wish to visit the museum, which can be accessed via the tourist office. On the outside wall of the church is a plaque commemorating the barn massacre and the unveiling of a memorial stone on November 3 1966.

Acknowledgements

In acknowledging those who have contributed to this book I must thank Paul Burke, not only for entrusting me with his own copy of *Ever Glorious*, but also in his placing of the Cheshire machine gun platoons and throwing some light on their subsequent actions on 28 May 1940. He has patiently answered my questions and provided me with a greater understanding of the Wormhout battlefield, in particular the probable fate of Lieutenant Basil Glasspool's 13 Platoon. Another WW2 Talk Forum member is Andy Newsome, who has demonstrated his usual generosity in providing me with the relevant war diaries and again answering my many questions. He visited Wormhout in 2012 and his online tour of the town has served to fill in many of the gaps in my own knowledge. To both of these individuals I offer my heartfelt thanks.

While recognizing the assistance given by the Public Records Office at Kew, the Imperial War Museum and the Army Museum, it is the accounts from officers and men who took part in the battle that really make the text come alive; and so to these men, sadly no longer with us, I extend my thanks for recording their impressions and experiences for later generations of researchers to read and digest.

I must thank Guy Rommelaere, whom I first bumped into by chance during a visit to Plaine au Bois, for allowing me to quote and use photographs from his book and for recently sending me two photographs of Wormhout as it was in 1940. The late Jon Cooksey was his usual encouraging self and remained quietly restrained when being constantly diverted to Second World War sites during our many visits to complete our most recent First World War guidebook. I also thank Pamela Langford at the Worcestershire and Mercian Regimental Museum for sending me relevant excerpts from Lieutenant Roger Cleverley's diary.

On the ground I have been accompanied by David Rowland and Paul Webster. Their company has made each visit thoroughly enjoyable and has contributed much to the suggested routes and the car tour found in Chapter 9. Paul's driving has made each trip a pleasure and made the sampling of different beers an essential part of each visit. Dave Roland's comments, usually from the back seat of the car, where he munches culinary delights away from prying eyes, have added a more restrained tone to the proceedings. Lastly, but by no means least, my wife Joan has tolerated my absence across the water with her usual understanding and tolerance and, despite her interests lying in another direction entirely, will probably be somewhat relieved that yet another Battleground Europe publication is in the hands of the publisher!

Apart from those photographs that I have privately sourced, the remainder has largely come from my personal collection. All mistakes in the text are entirely mine and while I have made every effort to trace copyright holders of the material used, I crave the indulgence of literary executors or copyright holders where these efforts have so far failed and would encourage them to contact me through the publisher so that any error can be rectified.

Chapter 1

The Dunkerque Corridor

The withdrawal of the British Expeditionary Force (BEF) to the Franco-Belgian frontier came as a surprise to those battalions that had been fighting on the line of the River Escaut. Captain 'Dick' Tomes, the 2/Warwicks' adjutant, wrote in his diary:

> We fully expected to return to the river (Escaut) within forty-eight hours and so our surprise and foreboding that something had gone very wrong was great when we were ordered to move back across the French frontier that night.

In command of the BEF was 53-year-old John Vereker, the 6th Viscount Gort, a man who was referred to more simply as Lord Gort. A highly decorated Grenadier Guards officer, he had served in the First World War with distinction, being awarded the Victoria Cross (VC) during the Battle of the Canal du Nord in 1918 whilst in command of the 1st Battalion. Commanding I Corps was General Sir John Dill, an individual who had served with distinction under Douglas Haig and succeeded Sir Edmund Ironside as Chief of the Imperial General Staff (CIGS) on 27 May 1940. After Dill's recall, command of I Corps passed to Lieutenant General Michael Barker. In command of II Corps was Lieutenant General Alan Brooke, a gunner officer who rose rapidly through the ranks in the First World War and was known for his energetic gusto and sometimes outspoken views. In January 1940 the first of the Territorial divisions arrived in France, giving rise to the formation of III Corps under the command of Lieutenant General Sir Robert Adam, a man who would shortly mastermind the evacuation of the BEF from Dunkerque.

The Allied front line on 25 May was approximately 130 miles in length, with the BEF holding 97 miles. On the previous day, 24 May, the tightly stretched Belgian front line between Menin and Courtrai collapsed under German pressure and a day later the Belgian armies were retreating in a northerly direction, opening up an 8 mile gap between them and the British north of the River Lys. Screened only by the armoured cars of the 12/Lancers, the Belgian collapse effectively left the road to Ypres wide open to units of the German Army Group B and raised fears that von Bock would launch an attack westward across the BEF's line of retreat, and link up with Army Group A in the Allied rear. Such fears were quite correct. On 28 May, forced into a small pocket along the River Lys, the Belgian King, Leopold III, and his military forces, surrendered unconditionally at

Lord Gort commanded the BEF in 1940.

4.00am. Belgian casualties during the eighteen day campaign numbered some 6,000 killed and 15,850 wounded.

On 25 May the 2/Warwicks were on Aubers Ridge and their two sister battalions in 143 Brigade, the 1/7 and 8 Warwicks, were at Sainghin and Fournes. The infamous Hitler Halt Order came into effect on 24 May and was not lifted until 26 May, effectively halting the German panzer divisions

Lieutenant General Alan Brooke commanded II Corps.

on the line of the canal running from Gravelines on the coast, through St-Omer, Béthune and La Bassée. While the order did not directly affect Wormhout and its environs, it did allow the BEF time to strengthen the Dunkerque Perimeter. Full details of this can be found in the Battleground Europe title *The Canal Line*. Elsewhere, events were moving at a faster pace; on the same day it become apparent that the hoped for break-out by Allied forces north of the River Somme to join up with the French across the neck of the panzer corridor to the south was, at best, a hopeless undertaking. To add to the difficulties already faced by Allied commanders, their forces north of the Somme were now practically enclosed by two German Army Groups: to the west Army Group A and, to the east, Army Group B. With this worsening situation unfolding before him, Lord Gort was told by the British Government that his principal task was to evacuate if necessary and salvage whatever he could of the BEF.

Since 14 May the British divisions, along with the French and Belgians, had been pushed back by the overwhelming power of the German forces and, with Whitehall realizing that evacuation was now a necessity, Lord Gort was ordered to prepare plans to evacuate the BEF. Fortunately, Gort had foreseen the order and preliminary plans were already in hand. Gort's creation of the Dunkerque Corridor allowed the bulk of the BEF to escape to Dunkerkque along a 17-mile wide passage, protected by those battalions and units deployed along the eastern and western edges of the corridor from Lille to Dunkerque. The French contribution at Lille to the evacuation taking place on the coast is often overlooked, but it was a vital part of the corridor created by Gort. On the night of 27/28 May, the BEF divisions near Lille were able to retreat over the river Lys but only III Corps of the French First Army, under the command of General René Prioux, managed to escape. The subsequent defence of Lille delayed the German advance for four days and occupied around seven German divisions, allowing the repatriation of much of the BEF from Dunkerque. This act of sacrifice by the French First Army, and its contribution to the evacuation, is often ignored by historians.

The corridor on the eastern edge ran from Lille, through Comines and north along the Ypres-Comines Canal to Nieuwport. In a movement that many historians regard as the order that saved the BEF from destruction, Gort dispatched the 5th and 50th Divisions to the canal to meet the threat from the east by units of *Generaloberst* Fedor von Bock's Army Group B (143 Brigade was attached to the 5th Division during this time). In the opinion of the author, had he not done so there may not have been a Dunkerque as we know it and the BEF would have been faced with a military disaster of gargantuan proportions. The handling of this flank was a military triumph for Brook and his commanders; the story of the BEF along the canal is recounted in the Battleground Europe title, *The Battle of the Ypres-Comines Canal 1940*.

North of Béthune the 2nd Division managed to hold German forces along the Lys until 27 May at huge cost to themselves. Some ninety-seven men of the 2/Royal Norfolks were murdered by the SS-*Totenkopf* at Le Paradis and a number of men of the 2/Durham Light Infantry were treated in a similar fashion at St-Venant by the SS-*Verfügungs*

As the defensive area gradually closed down from the south, the task facing the 48th Division, deployed south of Bergues and on the western side of the Dunkerque Corridor, was to hold the road that runs southward

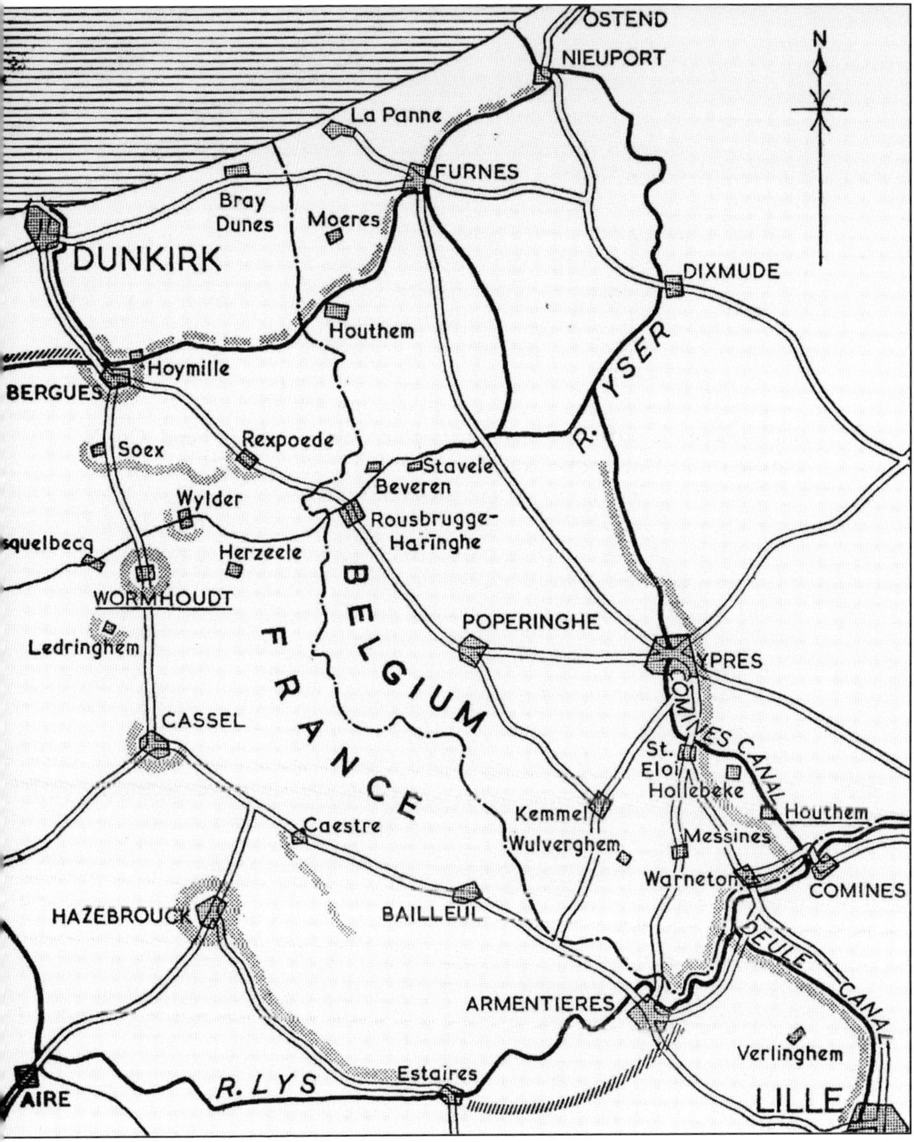

A map depicting the Dunkerque Corridor. The western flank ran from Lille through Cassel and Wormhout to Dunkerque, while the eastern flank took in the Ypres-Comines Canal before moving north along the Yser towards Nieuport and La Panne.

from Bergues through Wormhout, Cassel and Hazebrouck. Between Wormhout and Cassel, forward positions were occupied at Arnèke and Ledringhem to break up the attacking German forces.

At Cassel the 2/Gloucesters and 4/Ox and Bucks of 145 Brigade dug in and held the hilltop town successfully until ordered to breakout during the

Daily Express

Thursday, May 30, 1940

One Penny

Allies stem German onslaughts in history's greatest rearguard battle

B.E.F. FIGHTS DOWN NARROW CORRIDOR TO DUNKIRK

STOP PRESS

French stand-and-die troops battle in Lille

MARINES ENTRENCHED ALONG THE COAST

DOWN A RAPIDLY DWINDLING CORRIDOR, THIRTY MILES AT ITS WIDEST, THE B.E.F. AND ITS FRENCH ALLIES ARE SMASHING A WAY TO THE SEA THIS MORNING IN THE MOST GLORIOUS REARGUARD ACTION OF ANY WAR.

Two-thirds of the ports on which our armies in Flanders were based have fallen into enemy hands since the Belgian betrayal. Dunkirk remains, and it is towards this last link with England that the British troops are making their fighting withdrawal.

From now on the fate of the B.E.F., which has borne the brunt of battle for the last ten days, is largely dependent on the Navy and the R.A.F.

Already the R.A.F. have slowed down the German pursuit by plastering their lines with bombs and ground-strafing their advance troops. Over Dunkirk alone yesterday more than twenty enemy raiders were brought down by Defiants and Hurricanes.

Midnight reports pictured the B.E.F. fighting back in a compact wedge with its widest side on the thirty miles of coastline round Dunkirk.

HEROISM WORTHY OF TRADITIONS

LAST night's French communiqué stated:—

GALLANT ACTION

ENEMY ON HILLS

"SUPPLIES SATISFACTORY"

"CEASE FIRE!"

STRONG SUPPORT

"I.R.A. READY"

THE KING TO THE B.E.F.

Our hearts are with you

Lord Gort's reply:

SOVIET TURN DOWN CRIPPS TRADE VISIT

Will talk through Ambassador

French general jailed

Big air order transferred

Australia waives claim

After Quisling—

Captain Mutterer

TWO MORE BUDGETS

Lord Beaverbrook

German 'tourists'

The term Dunkerque Corridor was coined from the press coverage of the fighting that took place during late May in northern France. The reporting in the *Daily Express* was typical of the time.

night of 29 May. Thirteen men, under Second Lieutenant Julian Fane, eventually reached Dunkerque on 2 June and were amongst the last to be evacuated; the remainder were killed or captured. At Hazebrouck the more open nature of the town proved to be to the advantage of the German tanks and the defence of the town was distressingly short, the men of the 1/Ox and Bucks being overwhelmed within twenty-four hours on 28 May.

North of Cassel 143 Brigade were in place at Wormhout and resolutely defended the town until the afternoon of 28 May, when the order to withdraw saw the remnants moving north towards Bergues. Wormhout was also the scene of another massacre by the SS-*Liebstandarte*, in the course of which some hundred men were herded into a barn and the majority murdered.

The German forces of Army Group A slowly pushed north from Wormhout before running into Brigadier Norman's composite force, which had been dispatched from Cassel to respond to the threat south of Bergues. Here there was a short, sharp encounter in which the 1/Fife and Forfar Yeomanry and the 1/Welsh Guards, together with their supporting units, defended their sector south of Bergues until forced to withdraw late on 29 May. Nevertheless the German army found the BEF a tough nut to crack and its losses in tanks alone bear testament to the ferocity of the fighting during those final days of May. What the battalions defending the corridor had accomplished was a delaying action, which held the German forces long enough for the Dunkerque Perimeter to be put in place and defended. Without the sacrifice of those battalions there may not have been a Dunkerque evacuation as we know it.

Chapter 2

The German Order of Battle

The German Wehrmacht (and SS) regimental structure in 1940 was roughly similar in size to the British infantry brigade. Infantry regiments comprised three infantry battalions, each of which had three rifle companies plus a machine gun company with twelve heavy machine guns and six 81mm mortars. The pioneer platoon, signals platoon and the regimental band (used as stretcher bearers in combat) were directly attached to the regimental headquarters. The regimental artillery had two 150mm guns and six 75mm guns and the regimental anti-tank company had twelve 37mm anti-tank guns, four light machine guns and was often motorised. Unlike motorised divisions, the reconnaissance platoon was mounted on horses or bicycles.

The Motorised Infantry Division in May 1940

Whereas the standard infantry division relied heavily on horse drawn transport, the motorised division was fully mechanized and able to move at a much greater pace. The internal organization included two infantry regiments, an artillery regiment, a reconnaissance and a *panzerjäger* (tank hunter) battalion. As with the standard infantry division, it also had its own signals and pioneer battalions. In May 1940 it is likely the *panzerjäger* battalions were equipped with the *Panzerabwehrkanone* (Pak 3.7cm), as the Germans had no self-propelled tank hunters at the time.

20th Motorised Infantry Division (Wehrmacht)

The German 20th Infantry Division was established in 1934 but did not assume its bona-fide designation until the creation of the Wehrmacht was announced in October 1935. In the autumn of 1937 it was upgraded to a fully motorised division. As the 20th Motorised Infantry, Division, the unit took part in the invasion of Poland as part of Heinz Guderian's XIX Corps, where, as with other motorised divisions, it was found to be a little cumbersome. Reduced in size by about a third to six motorised infantry battalions organized into two regiments, plus the standard divisional support units, it took part in the invasion of France and remained there until April 1941. Commanded by 57-year-old *General der Infantrie* Mauritz von Wiktorin, the division had been present at Arras on 21May as part of Army Group A before moving north to Dunkerque via Wormhout. In 1944 age forced Wiktorin's discharge from the army and he died twelve years later, in 1956. In July 1943 the division was redesignated the 20th Panzergrenadier Division.

General der Infantrie **Mauritz von Wiktorin on the left, with Heinz Guderian and General Semyon Krivoshein.**

At Arnèke and Ledringhem Infantry Regiment 90 (IR 90) was commanded by *Oberst* Dietricht Kraiss, who was wounded in early August 1944 whilst in command of the 352nd Division in Normandy and he died on 6 August 1944. IR 76, commanded by 48-year-old *Generalmajor* Hans Gollnick, appears not to have been involved in the fighting in Arnèke and Ledringhem. After the Gloucesters had been overwhelmed, units of the Division moved north to engage the Worcesters around Bambecque and Rexpoëde.

2 Panzer Division (Wehrmacht)

In May 1940 the 2nd Panzer Division was fighting under the command of XIX Panzer Corps and was the first Panzer division to reach the English

Oberst **Dietricht Kraiss was in command of IR 90 at Ledringhem.**

Generalleutnant **Rudolf Veiel.**

Channel. on 20 May 1940. Formed in October 1935, under the command of Heinz Guderian, the Division was one of the first tank divisions to be formed. In 1938 it took part in the annexation of Austria and by the start of the war in 1939 most of the establishment were Austrians. Suffering heavy losses in Poland during the 1939 invasion, it went on to see combat in France and Flanders during 1940, where it was part of Guderian's XIX Corps. At Wormhout the Division was commanded by *Generalleutnant* Rudolf Veiel. In 1944 he was relieved of the command of Battle Sector V because of alleged complicity in the 20 July conspiracy to assassinate Adolf Hitler; on 16 April 1945 he was put in the Officer Reserve (*Führerreserve*) of the Army High Command. After surrendering, Veiel spent two years in American captivity and was released in 1947. He died in 1956.

The Division was sent to Russia in October 1941 and was eventually thrown back by the Soviet winter offensive of 1941–42, then taking part in the defensive fighting in the Rzhev Salient and in the battles of Kursk, Orel, Yelnja and Kiev during the winter of 1943-4. Withdrawn to Amiens, in France, it was drawn into the Battle of Normandy, breaking out at Falaise with severe losses, to be reformed in September 1944. The Ardennes Offensive (Battle of the Bulge) was the last major campaign in which the Division was involved before it surrendered to the Americans in April 1945.

(*Left*) *Oberst* Heinrich Gabler was in command of the 3/Panzer Regiment. (*Right*) The 4/Panzer Regiment was under the command of *Oberst* Hans Voigt.

A German battle map indicates that it was principally elements of the 2nd Panzer Brigade, 3/Panzer Regiment, under *Oberst* Heinrich Gabler, that were engaged at Wormhout and Ledringhem; while 4/Panzer Regiment, under *Oberst* Hans Voigt, was deployed to the north west of Wormhout, towards West-Cappel. According to Guderian's Corps Movement Order No 15, the Division was relieved by the 9th Panzer Division on 29/30 May in preparation for the drive south of the Somme.

The Rise of the Waffen-SS

The Waffen-SS was the armed wing of the Nazi Party's SS-organization and grew from three regiments to over thirty-eight divisions during the Second World War, serving alongside the regular army. The *Leibstandarte Adolf Hitler* (LSAH) was formed from SS volunteers in March 1933 under the command of *Gruppenführer* Otto 'Sepp' Dietrich and was originally created as a personal bodyguard for Adolf Hitler. In August 1939 Hitler placed the *Leibstandarte* under the operational control of the Army High Command. In spite of the swift military victory over Poland in September 1939, the regular army felt that the performance of the SS units left much to be desired; they took unnecessary risks and had a higher casualty rate than the army. For example, at Pabianice, the LSAH had to be rescued by an army regiment after it was surrounded by Polish units; although, in its defence, Sepp Deitrich maintained it had been hampered by having to fight piecemeal instead of as one formation and was improperly equipped by the army to carry out its objectives. What soon became clear, however, was the number of war crimes committed against the Polish people by the LSAH, who became notorious for the torching of villages without military justification and for atrocities against civilians in numerous towns.

***Gruppenführer* Otto 'Sepp' Dietrich.**

In October 1939 the SS regiments *Deutschland*, *Germania* and *Der Führer* were reorganised into the *SS-Verfügungs* Division and Hitler further authorised the creation of two new divisions, the *SS-Totenkopf* Division and the *Polizei* Division, the latter formed from members of the national police force. It was men from the *SS-Totenkopf*, under *Hauptsturmführer* Fritz Knoechlein, that was responsible for murdering ninety-nine men of the 2/Royal Norfolks on 27 May 1940 at Le Paradis.

At the end of 1939 the LSAH remained an independent formation and was increased in strength to create a reinforced motorised regiment, spending the winter of 1939 and the spring of 1940 training and preparing for the coming war in the west. In May they moved to the front and were attached to the 227th Infantry Division. Hitler next authorised the creation of four motorised artillery battalions in March 1940, one for each division and the LSAH. The German high command was supposed to supply these new battalions with artillery but was reluctant to hand over guns from its own arsenal. The weapons arrived only slowly and by the time of the Battle of France only the *Leibstandarte* regiment was up to strength. On 10 May the LSAH overcame Dutch border guards to spearhead the German advance of X Corps into the Netherlands and entered Rotterdam and the Hague, which they reached on 15 May, capturing 3,500 Dutch soldiers as prisoners of war. After the Dutch surrender, the LSAH moved south to France on 24 May. Becoming part of XIX Panzer Corps, under the command of Heinz Guderian, they took up a position 15 miles south west of Dunkirk along the line of the Aa Canal, facing the Allied defensive line near Watten. Their next objective was Wormhout.

The Leibstandarte Adolf Hitler (LSAH)

After being reformed as a Panzer Grenadier formation in 1942, it returned to the Eastern Front in 1943, under the command of *Brigadeführer*

Waffen-SS troops.

Theodor Wisch, where it suffered heavy casualties at Kharkov, prompting its transfer to northern Italy for refitting. It was a short stay and the Division soon found itself in Russia again, where it was involved in heavy combat around Kiev and tried unsuccessfully to prevent the encirclement of the First Panzer Army. After suffering heavy losses at Skala, it was transferred to the west, fighting at Caen and Mortain in Normandy, before breaking out of the Falaise Pocket by the skin of its teeth. Michael Wittmann was one of the better known tank commanders of the Division at this time and, by the day of his death in August 1944, he was credited with 135 tank kills, 120 of which were accomplished on the Eastern Front. The Division was again rebuilt in time to see combat in the Ardennes Offensive (Battle of the Bulge). In July 1944 the Division came under the command of *Standartenführer* Wilhelm Mohnke, who was widely thought to have given the order for the murder of the British troops at Wormhout. Escaping a trial for the Wormhout Massacre, Mohnke surrendered to the Russians in Berlin and remained in captivity until October 1955. He died, aged ninety, in 2001.

Along with a number of other SS formations, the LSAH had been reformed into smaller, fast-moving *Kampfgruppen* (or battle groups) as preparation for the Ardennes offensive. As part of *Kampfgruppe* Joachim Peiper, they succeeded in making rapid initial progress during the offensive but became deeply implicated in the murder of American prisoners at Malmedy, a crime for which Peiper was sentenced to death in 1947. Commuted to life imprisonment, he was released in 1956 and died in mysterious circumstances in France when his house burned down in July 1976. Concluding its war in Hungary, the Division took part in the unsuccessful Lake Balaton counter attack before ending the war on the southern sector of the Eastern Front, with *Gruppenführer* Otto Kumm in command. Surviving the war, Kumm died in 2004.

Throughout its existence the LSAH was embroiled in accusations of murder of military and civilian prisoners alike, with that of Wormhout

***Obersturmbannführer* Joachim Peiper.**

***Gruppenführer* Otto Kumm.**

***Obersturmbannführer* Martin Kohlröser commanded the 1/LSAH.**

being one of many atrocities. In May 1940 the LSAH comprised three infantry battalions, each consisting of four motorised companies containing approximately 250 officers and men. The 1/Battalion LSAH, commanded by *Obersturmbannführer* Martin Kohlröser, were on the left flank roughly north of the Esquelbecq road attacking towards La Belle Vue on the D916, the 2/Battalion LSAH, commanded by *Sturmbannführer* Ernst Schützeck, were in the centre attacking Wormhout and the 3/Battalion, which was held in reserve behind the 1/Battalion LSAH, was under the command of *Obersturmbannführer* Wilhelm Trabant. In addition to the anti-tank company, there was also a motorcycle company, along with engineers and signals and an artillery company. From Wormhout the *Leibstandarte* pursued the retreating British to Bambecque and reached Rexpoëde on 30 May. Corps Movement Order No. 15 from Guderian's headquarters at Château Louches, in the Pas-de-Calais, reached the LSAH Headquarters at the Chemin de Helle, at Wylder, late that day, ordering them to move to a new area of responsibility south west of Calais.

Infantry Regiment *Großdeutschland*

In the first week of 1939, Hitler ordered that the *Wach Regiment Berlin* be renamed *Infanterie Regiment Großdeutschland*, giving the unit a permanent cadre and, unlike other regiments of the German Army, the recruits of the *Großdeutschland* were to be drawn from across the nation. The regiment is sometimes mistakenly understood to be part of the Waffen-SS, probably because it wore distinctive cuff titles of the type granted to Waffen-SS units. Whether this distinction led to the regiment not becoming involved in a number of atrocities against civilians is doubtful; the first recorded incident of its murderous activity was during the rout of the French Army in June 1940, when they murdered African soldiers and their white officers near the Bois d' Eraine (Oise). Ten more black Frenchmen were reportedly murdered by its members near Lyon.

In 1942 it was expanded into the *Großdeutschland* Division, the best equipped division in the Wehrmacht; it received equipment before all other units, including some Waffen SS units. It received its final name, *Panzergrenadier-Regiment Großdeutschland*, in 1943. In May 1940 the regiment was under the command of 49-year-old *Oberstleutnant* Wilhelm

A forward command post. Although it was a Wehrmacht unit, the *Großdeutschland* regiment wore cuff titles that are normally associated with SS units.

Hunold von Stockhausen. It avoided Wormhout, advancing on the left flank towards the high ground west of Socx, along with units of the 2nd Panzer Division. It is possible that units of the regiment were in action against the 1/F&F Yeomanry and the Welsh Guards at Vywfcg and West-Cappel. Von Stockhausen died in 1964.

Chapter 3

The British Order of Battle

Below is a guide to the composition of the formations referred to in the text; smaller units have been omitted. It should be remembered that after a fighting withdrawal that began after 14 May, almost every battalion involved in the defence of the Western Dunkerque Corridor was by no means at full strength or in possession of the full quota of armament.

A **British infantry brigade** had a headquarters company and three infantry battalions, with artillery support provided by the allocation of a machine gun company, anti tank battery and artillery regiment as required. The **British infantry battalion**, numbering at full strength an average of 780 men, consisted of a battalion headquarters, a headquarters company (signals and administration platoons), four rifle companies, a support company with a carrier platoon, mortar platoon, anti tank platoon and pioneer platoon. The rifle platoon had a headquarters, which in theory included a 2-inch mortar and an anti tank weapon team, and three rifle sections, supported by a three-man Bren gun team. In May 1940, a **British infantry division** was organized into three brigades and numbered about 13,600 officers and men. The division had at its disposal a machine gun battalion and three field artillery regiments equipped with either 4.5-inch howitzers or 25/18-pdrs.

144 Infantry Brigade

The brigade was one of three assigned to the 48th (South Midland) Division, a territorial formation that landed in France in January 1940 under the command of 55-year-old Major General Andrew Thorne, an officer who took over from Major General Frank Roberts in December 1939.

During the latter end of May 1940 the division found itself defending three separate locations along the western and eastern edges of the Dunkerque Corridor; to the east 143 Brigade, commanded by Brigadier James Muirhead, was defending the line of the Ypres-Comines Canal, to the west 145 Brigade, under Brigadier Nigel Somerset, was at Cassel and Hazebrouck while Brigadier James Hamilton's 144 Brigade was at Ledringhem and Wormhout, a mere 5 miles north of Cassel along the D916.

The 55-year-old James 'Hammy' Hamilton was described as having an unforgettable personality and, despite being over fifty, was physically fit and had the ability of knowing the right time to praise and the right time to rebuke. Famous for his grin, he was reportedly fearless and in possession of an uncanny anticipation of the enemy's movements. All of these characteristics would be needed over the coming days.

Major General Andrew Thorne.

On 22/23 May the brigade withdrew from its positions along the Escaut and found itself in Dunkerque two days later, with Brigade HQ opening at Rousbrugge, some 8 miles south east of Dunkerque. Ordered south, Second Lieutenant 'Bill' Haywood, the brigade intelligence officer at the time, was sent ahead to Le Briel to find a suitable building for Brigade Headquarters and wrote of his irritation on discovering that Brigade Headquarters had opened in the Château Maes on the D55 Wylder road at Wormhout.

Château Maes was a rectangular red brick building, described by Haywood as ugly, with an asphalt courtyard, several outbuildings and belonged to a Belgian industrialist. The rooms were richly furnished and the grounds were extensive, enabling the brigade transport to shelter from aerial observation beneath the trees. Haywood describes a 'shallow, ornamental lake, on which floated two hungry, angry and suspicious swans. There was also in the garden a peacock with a raucous voice, apparently a victim of insomnia.' Private Lou Carrier became victim to the peacock's scream when, initially thinking a colleague had been hit, he raised his rifle to dispatch the bird but was told by an irate lieutenant that

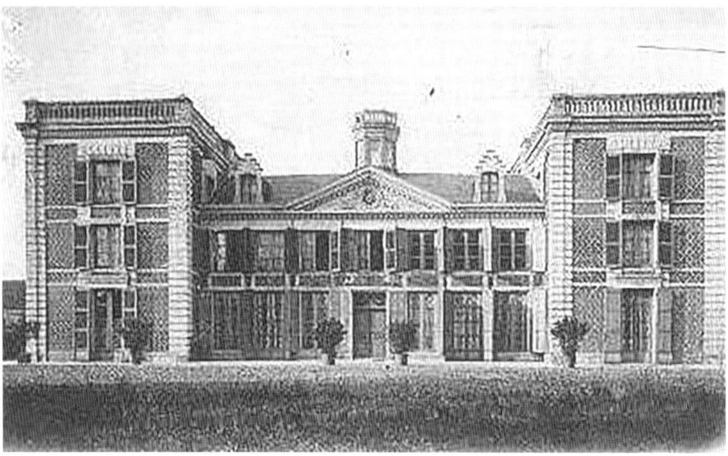

144 Brigade Headquarters was in Château Maes, Wormhout.

it was unlucky to shoot peacocks. The lieutenant may well have been Haywood but the end result was predictable, for as soon as the officer had moved out of sight we are told that Carrier shot the bird and, as he said afterwards, if shooting a peacock brought bad luck, he never noticed it! On 28 May, after the fighting in Wormhout had almost ceased, Brigade Headquarters moved north to Rexpoëde in the midst of a heavy rainstorm; it was to be a short stay as at 8.30am the next day Hamilton moved to a farm near Killem, a mere 9 miles from Bray Dunes. By the early hours of 31 May embarkation was completed and the survivors of the brigade were on their way home to England.

5/Gloucesters

Although the Battalion, a Territorial unit, was initially affected by a virulent influenza epidemic prior to embarkation to France; it eventually arrived in France with twenty-five officers and some 600 other ranks on 15 January 1940. The battalion arrived in Wormhout during the late afternoon of 25 May.

The Battalion, under the command of Lieutenant Colonel Guy Buxton, deployed each company astride a main road, whilst Buxton established his headquarters amongst the brick kilns near Rue de l'Ancienne Abbaye in Wormhout. The war diary informs us that companies were in position by dark. On 25 May the battalion was ordered by Hamilton to move south to the two villages of Arnèke and Ledringhem, which were to be held for twenty-four hours. Ledringhem was first occupied by Second Lieutenant Shephard and the carrier platoon and then by C and D Companies

The 5/Gloucesters Headquarters Company. Front row from the left: Guy Buxton, Brigadier Hamilton, French liaison officer, Major Priestly and the Rev Gethin Jones. Standing behind Buxton is Captain Flowers RAMC.

(Captain Mason and Captain Rockett), who were in turn relieved by the 2/Warwicks. The carriers then moved into Arnèke and were followed by A and B companies (Captain Dennis Biddle and Captain Charles Norris). Biddle was later to command the 2/Gloucesters on D Day 1944. Company positions were consolidated and Buxton established Battalion Headquarters in the *Mairie* at Ledringhem, along with Major Anthony Waller and Headquarters Company.

2/Warwicks

The Battalion disembarked in France on 24 September 1939 under the command of Lieutenant Colonel Piers Dunn. He was evacuated with a burst ulcer on 21 May, command devolving to the battalion's second in command, Major Phillip 'Pip' Hicks; and it was Hicks who brought the battalion to Wormhout.

The only regular battalion in the brigade, they arrived in Wormhout during the early hours of the morning of 26 May in the pouring rain. The town was more or less undamaged as the Warwicks established their company positions and Battalion Headquarters was opened in the Château Morael, with the Regimental Aid Post (RAP) in a large house between the headquarters building and the transport, which was concealed beneath trees.

Major Phillip Hicks, taken as a brigadier at the Hartstein Hotel, Arnhem, in 1944.

C Company was sent to occupy Esquelbecq, a small, pretty village, about 3 miles to the west of Wormhout. It was with some dismay that they were withdrawn on 27 May to provide a guard for the 48th Divisional Headquarters at Bergues. Consequently, B Company (Captain Edward Jerram) became responsible for the area north and south of the Esquelbecq road, A Company (Major Cecil Chichester-Constable) was in the centre and D Company (Captain Frazer Lynn-Allen) held the area from the Ledringhem road to the road from Cassel. Thus, the three remaining companies of Warwicks were now responsible for the defence of the western half of the town while the eastern half was the responsibility of the 8/Worcesters. But, as the German attack was probably coming from the west and south west, it was the Warwicks who would bear the brunt of the encounter. The guns of the 53/Anti-Tank Regiment and the machine guns of the 4/Cheshires were dispersed amongst the Warwicks' companies, which averaged eighty to ninety men in each company.

8/Worcesters

The Battalion arrived in France on 16 January 1940 under the command of Lieutenant Colonel James Johnstone. It moved to Wormhout during the night of 26 May. Although officially in brigade reserve, the Battalion was deployed to protect the roads leading north towards Dunkerkque from marauding AFVs advancing from Calais.

Battalion Headquarters was opened in Château Maes on the D55 Wylder road. A Company was deployed to the Kicken Put and the Rietveld area and B Company (Major Frank Ramsay) to Oudzeele. D Company (Captain John Farrar) was at Wylder and C Company, (Captain Grahame Macdonald) was held in brigade reserve at Château Maes, while Johnstone opened Battalion Headquarters in a gardener's cottage in the grounds of Château Maes.

Early on 28 May the rapid movement of German forces demanded a quick rethink and the companies south of Wormhout were withdrawn. A Company and Lieutenant Anslow was moved to join D Company at Wylder, where John Farrar assumed command of both bodies of men; and B Company was moved to the south east of Wormhout, before joining the Battalion in its withdrawal north to Bambecque.

53 (Worcester Yeomanry) Anti-Tank Regiment

This Territorial regiment was equipped with 2lb solid shot anti-tank guns. It was under the command of Lieutenant Colonel Edgar Medley. It arrived in France during the early part of January 1940 and had the dubious honour of being among the first Territorial regiments to be sent to France. Divided into four batteries, 209 was stationed at Kidderminster, 210 and 212 were stationed at Kings Heath and 211 was stationed at Bewdley. As with many such regiments, each company was deployed to support a particular battalion or brigade. Thus on 26 May, 209/Battery was at Cassel

Men of the 53/Anti-Tank Regiment manhandle a 2-Pounder in training near Thirsk.

under Major Ronald Cartland, 210/Battery was at Wormhout and Ledringhem, one troop from 211/Battery was sent to Cassel under Major Henry Mercer on 28 May to reinforce 209/Battery, while H and I troops were deployed in Wormhout under the command of 210/Battery and Major Wiggin. 212/Battery was with Usherforce and under the orders of the 2nd Division at Beignes. At Wormhout, Regimental Headquarters was at Château Morael, with the 2/Warwicks. A full description of the rearguard action at Cassel can be read in the Battleground Europe publication, *Cassel and Hazebrouck 1940*.

4/Cheshire Regiment

The Battalion was under the command of Lieutenant Colonel Ray Danson and divided into four companies of machine gunners, each company being equipped with twelve heavy .303 machine guns. By 26 May A and

A heavy Vickers machine gun and crew of the Cheshires on manoeuvres in England.

C Companies had been combined and sent to Cassel to reinforce 145 Brigade, B Company was in the Ledringhem-Wylder area under the command of Major Ashton and D Company was at La Panne under Major Kissack. On 27 May most of the Battalion, less A and C Companies, was placed under the command of 144 Brigade; and D Company was attached to the 2/Warwicks at Wormhout. D Company included Captain Sir John Nicholson, 13 Platoon under Lieutenant Basil Glasspool, 14 Platoon under Second Lieutenant Merlin-Davies and 15 Platoon under Second Lieutenant Ravenscroft. The company was strengthened by the addition of Lieutenant Geoffrey Clemence and 8 Platoon from B Company.

It is fortunate that we have been given some insight into the deployment of the Cheshires by Major Harry Kissack's account of D Company at Wormhout:

> It was decided to place machine guns in the forward defended localities of B Company, 2/Warwicks. 13 Platoon on the left and 14 Platoon on the right had good fields of fire, due west for about 1,500 yards. 15 Platoon in the centre were 3–400 yards behind the crest and could fire over the crest using observation from trees in gun positions. Platoons were in position by about 1900 hours. About 19.30 hrs 14 Platoon were relieved by 8 Platoon.

Danson initially established Battalion Headquarters at Herzeele.

24/Field Regiment, Royal Artillery

The regiment arrived in Cherbourg on 23 September 1939 under the command of Lieutenant Colonel William Crowe, who remained in command until 24 March. Major HJV Beddington, from18/Field Regiment, was promoted to lieutenant colonel and took over the regiment.

On 26 May 50/70 Battery was situated between Wormhout and Herzeele on the right and 22/56 Battery was near Rietveld on the left, the batteries of 18/25-pounders covering the 2/Warwicks at Wormhout and the 5/Gloucesters at Arnèke respectively . Observation posts were established in the church towers and Regimental Headquarters were at Château Maes with 144 Brigade.

On 28 May large numbers of tanks and infantry were engaged by Captain Rowlandson, who was observing from the gendarmerie in Wormhout. At the same time Captain Robinson was engaging enemy AFVs and infantry between Cassel and Ledringhem. After the Warwicks began to withdraw from Wormhout both batteries were ordered to the Killem area. An observation post under Captain Rowlandson was established in Bambecque, which remained in position until enemy tanks entered the village from the west.

1/Welsh Guards

The Battalion arrived in Marseilles from Gibraltar, under the command of Lieutenant Colonel Felix Copeland-Griffiths, on 7 November 1939 and

A 25-pounder field gun, typical of those used by 24/Field Regiment, in action during an exercise in December 1939.

A Mark V1 light tank of C Squadron 2/F&F Yeomanry in Northern Ireland, June 1940. The 1/F&F Yeomanry would have been equipped with the same vehicles.

was immediately deployed to provide protection for GHQ at Arras and Harbaraq. Deployed during the defence of Arras, the Battalion arrived in the town on 17 May and during its time there saw the fourth VC of the campaign awarded posthumously to Lieutenant Christopher Furness. On 26 May the Battalion took over the defence of Mont des Récollects at Cassel and on 29 May it moved north to Vyfweg as part of Brigadier Norman's composite brigade.

1/Fife and Forfar Yeomanry

The Regiment was one of three that were allocated to form the 1/Armoured Reconnaissance Brigade in March 1940 under the command of Brigadier Charles Norman. The brigade consisted of two Territorial units, the 1/F&F Yeomanry and the 1/East Riding Yeomanry, together with the regular troops of the 13th/18th Hussars, a regiment that never joined the Brigade and was destined to support the troops defending the Ypres-Comines Canal. The 1/F&F Yeomanry was under the command of Lieutenant Colonel Ronald 'Ponto' Sharp and equipped with light tanks and Carden-Lloyd carriers. After moving to Cassel on 24 May, it took up duties as part of the garrison defending the hilltop town; but it was to be a short deployment as on 28 May, leaving the 1/East Riding Yeomanry at Cassel, Sharp was ordered by Norman to move north with the Welsh Guards to Vyfweg (Le Cing Chemins), where German tanks and infantry were reportedly penetrating the western edge of the Dunkerque Corridor. Norman established his headquarters near the crossroads at Vyfweg.

Chapter 4

The 5/Gloucesters at Arnèke and Ledringhem

26–29 May 1940

The plan to occupy the two villages of Arnèke and Ledringhem was made in consultation with Hamilton's overall strategy. He assumed, correctly as it turned out, that Arnèke, being the most westerly part of his line of defence, would be attacked first. The plan allowed for the two companies deployed in the village to fall back on Ledringhem before they were overwhelmed. In this manner he hoped that the infantry and armoured vehicles of the German 20th Motorised Division would be held long enough to prevent them from moving north too quickly and possibly joining the SS *Liebstandarte* Infantry.

The Deployment at Arnèke and Ledringhem

At Arnèke the forward southern position was held by D Company, supported by three 25mm anti-tank guns from the brigade anti-tank company under Second Lieutenant Goscomb, while Second Lieutenant Henn, with 11 Platoon, was positioned on the railway line to the north of the village. The centre and northern parts of the village were held by A Company on either side of the railway line. As we know, Captain Mason's C Company was covering the road junctions on the D52 between Arnèke and Ledringhem; but they were without Second Lieutenant Liversidge's platoon, who was deployed to Rietveld to form a roadblock on the D916. It appears that an 'advanced' platoon of the 4/Cheshires, commanded by Second Lieutenant Paddy Woodhouse, was also present in Ledringhem. We know that Woodhouse was wounded and captured in the village; but there is no mention of the Cheshires in any other reports.

In Ledringhem itself, Buxton established Battalion Headquarters in the *Mairie,* situated at the junction of Chemnin de Bodeye with Route d'Arnèke, and he positioned Headquarters Company to the south and west of the village and around the *Mairie*. B Company was given the task of defending the eastern flank and northern end of the village. Battalion transport was mainly dispersed in the orchard on the east side of the village, where today a housing estate has been built. The battalion was given the support of 24/Field Artillery Regiment and to provide targeting information a Forward Observation Officer (FOO) took up residence in the church tower. **27 May** The news that armoured fighting vehicles (AFV)

An aerial photograph of Ledringhem. The church and its churchyard are visible on the left, while the *Mairie* is just out of frame on the left of the church. The main street can be seen behind the church.

had been observed to the east and south of Arnèke indicated that German forces had broken through the French and were now moving north towards Dunkerque. Heavy bursts of mortar fire pointed towards an enemy incursion, which prompted Buxton to send a carrier section under Sergeant Brown to investigate. Brown successfully ambushed groups of enemy soldiers who had crossed the railway line and were now making a determined attack on the village, while Lieutenant Donald Norris from D Company effectively dealt with another large concentration of enemy. Norris was wounded the next day and died as a prisoner of war in August 1942; he is buried at Hanover War Cemetery.

As the fighting spread into the village a burst of machine-gun fire wounded Major Biddle, CSM Hill of A Company and Captain Rockett of D Company; at around the same time Lieutenant Michael Shephard's remaining carriers were ordered into Arnèke from Ledringhem in order to prevent an organized attack on Arnèke from the southern and northern flanks. Having successfully beaten back the enemy attack, the carriers brought up fresh supplies of ammunition as the enemy withdrew from the village. A definite lull in the fighting allowed the wounded to be evacuated and the dwindling Arnèke garrison to be concentrated in the north of the village. A and D Companies were brought back to the C Company area under the cover of darkness. Unfortunately, Second Lieutenant Henn's

11 Platoon was unable to be contacted and only rejoined the battalion at Rexpoëde.

Withdrawal to Ledringhem

At this point in the battle there was a distinct possibility of Arnèke being cut off and consequently Buxton ordered the three companies to withdraw across the D52 to Ledringhem, leaving behind an enemy that had lost some five tanks and a number of armoured cars.

Only one gun from 53/Anti-Tank Regiment was brought back to Ledringhem from Arnèke. It was reinforced subsequently by another gun from 211/Battery, a move that coincided with Lieutenant George Rodwell being wounded in the leg. For his actions at this time he was awarded the Military Cross, which was gazetted in August 1940. At 4.00am on 28 May the artillery of 24/Field Regiment opened fire and continued firing for most of the morning on all likely areas of enemy concentration.

For the Gloucesters, now deployed in all round defence at Ledringhem, the situation was becoming somewhat desperate, particularly as further orders had been received for the Battalion to hold their positions for a further twenty-four hours. Sergeant Ivor Organ recalled a German vehicle crashing into a roadblock at Ledringhem:

> A few second later we heard explosions and ran into the village; the front of the enemy vehicle was embedded in a makeshift barricade and a few yards further on a pretty big German was lying on the ground. He had taken a bullet in the head and his brains were spilling out. We all felt sick!

During the day the enemy, working around both flanks of the village, effectively surrounded the Gloucesters and, despite Private Albert Joines making five rather hazardous trips to Brigade Headquarters by motor cycle, contact with Château Maes was finally severed at about midday.

Enemy artillery and mortar fire killed one of the observers in the church tower and severely damaged the centre of the village, the church and several outlying farms and houses as well as the old Guilleman windmill, which was destroyed by a German incendiary bomb. Sergeant Organ again:

> We quickly realised that by setting the houses alight the enemy were going to force us out into the open. The flames were so high that we soon saw them running towards us. We opened fire and each time I fired a round the enemy retaliated, blowing out doors and windows.

Although the enemy was seen by the church near to Battalion Headquarters, apparently massing for an attack, no advance was made until dusk, a situation that did not appear to bother Captain Flowers, the battalion medical officer, who continued to treat the wounded in the cellars of the *Mairie*.

Orders to Withdraw

This is the point at which the two lance corporals from Lieutenant Liversidge's platoon made their entrance to the village and arrived at the *Mairie* at Ledringhem. The reader will recall that this platoon had been deployed to Rietveld and then withdrawn by Hamilton to Brigade Headquarters. With all communication links destroyed, Lance Corporals Ernest Barnfield and Reginald Mayo volunteered to take the order to withdraw to Ledringhem. Without the timely arrival of the two men, the Gloucesters would have fought on until they had been overrun. The war diary recorded the event:

> As the attack was developing two runners arrived in the village with a message from brigade: 'Make your way after dark, or when you can, to Bambecque via Herzeele. At Bambecque will try to contact you. We are hard pressed here and hope to get away after dark to Wylder or Bambecque.'

Barnfield and Mayo were awarded the Military Medal for their journey across country. Mayo was later hit in the hip and had a leg amputated while still a prisoner of war.

For Buxton the order to withdraw was easier given than executed. All the carriers and anti-tank guns had been put out of action, with most of the

MILITARY MEDALLIST MARRIED AT ALL SAINTS'

The bridal party leaving All Saints' Church last week after the wedding of Pte. Jack Barnfield, M.M., R.A.O.C., only son of Mr. and Mrs. A. Barnfield, of 33, Avon-road, Cheltenham, to Miss Dorothy M. Keen, only daughter of Mrs. H. Keen, of 18, Hazelwood-road, Acocks Green, Birmingham. The bridegroom was one of the first Cheltenham men to win the Military Medal in this war.

A newspaper cutting from 1942 reporting the marriage of Private Jack Barnfield to Dorothy Keen.

gun crews now casualties, and it was becoming increasingly difficult to link up with the remnants of the company and section posts. Two attempts were made to pull out of the village but both were foiled by German infantry attacks. The cancellation of zero hour unfortunately did not reach the greater part of C Company, who withdrew as ordered under Captain Welford and found themselves prisoners of war.

The war diary of IR 90 indicated that it was its 9/*Kompanie* that was attacking the western edge of Ledringhem:

> Since this *kompanie* had great difficulty in reaching the Roman road that afternoon, the assault was called off in order to avoid huge losses and re-scheduled for the evening. At 21.00 hrs the *kompanie* resumed the attack from the west and south west, preceded by a preliminary barrage from the 2nd Battalion, 20th Artillery Regiment.

As the enemy entered the churchyard and attempted to advance down the village street they were prevented from doing so by Bren gun fire. However, they did manage to establish themselves in the houses at the far end until they were driven out by three successful counter attacks. These attacks resulted in three officers being badly wounded, and two brothers, Second Lieutenant Donald Norris and his elder brother Captain Charles Norris, together with Lieutenant Anthony Dewsnap, had eventually to be left behind, unable to manage the breakout to Bambecque.

Two of these counter attacks involved Lieutenant Michael Shephard, who won a Military Cross that was gazetted in August 1940. He was wounded in the head during the second attack but has left a description of the first attack:

> Seven officers and seven men with rifles and bayonets and a few hand grenades, and two men with Bren guns, prepared to attack the enemy 150 yards away. We waited by the wall of the HQ and in the ditch on the other side of the road. Then we spread out and began moving down the street … It was natural we should take up some sort of war cry: 'Up the Gloucesters!', and shout encouraging words to each other, at the same time gaining confidence as we moved forward … The burning buildings cast an eerie glow against the church walls and proved to be of assistance to us, for we were able to see the Germans cross the street ahead of us. They gave us a rather feeble volley, which was returned wholeheartedly by our rifles fired from the hip, and on we went.

Shortly before the battalion broke out the enemy called on the services of a company of the 20/Pioneer Battalion, which sent up a flame thrower, the fuel of which did not ignite. The unfortunate operator was disposed of quite quickly but the defending Gloucesters were covered in a residue of oil, giving rise to a temporary gas alarm.

Breakout

The withdrawal was finally set for 1.00am on 29 May but before that could happen there was one further tragedy that was to beset the battalion. Having already been dispatched by Buxton to clear the churchyard, 34-year-old Major Anthony Waller then went with Buxton to investigate a reported incursion by the enemy at the back of the *Mairie*. Both officers were wounded by a burst of automatic fire; Major Waller was hit in the head and Buxton in the leg.

Sergeant Organ remembered the incident:

> The colonel sent me with a dozen men to hold a trench behind the *Mairie*. No sooner had we jumped down than the Huns opened fire. Then we heard shouts and screams from behind a copse: Two of our men were down. For one of them there was nothing we could do ... The soldier who we had just brought in was none other than Major Waller, who soon after breathed his last, his head was a bloody mass. Returning to the trench I saw that during my absence a grenade had wounded all the men there.

Waller was the most senior officer to be killed at Ledringhem. For many of the Gloucesters dug in around the *Mairie*, the chances of being able to escape successfully must have looked poor. Fortunately, a lull in the fighting gave Buxton the chance he had been waiting for and allowed what was left of the battalion to leave the village undetected.

Two medical orderlies were left behind with the badly wounded officers and men while the remainder of the battalion, including Captain Robinson, his party from 24/Field Regiment and the medical officer, moved off from the orchard at 1.15am. Their way was illuminated by the burning Guillemin windmill. Thirteen officers and 139 men, many of whom were wounded, headed off in single file towards Herzeele, with Captain Leslie Hauting, the battalion's adjutant, ensuring the column kept on course. [Hauting died, probably of malaria, in March 1944 while seconded to the West African Reconnaissance Regiment in Nigeria.]

The progress to Herzeele was painfully slow but not without incident, as the regimental historian recorded:

> At one time they came across a party of sleeping Germans, stopped to take an officer and two men prisoner without waking the others, and went on. Going through a hamlet, they saw Germans sleeping in the houses. A pair of farm horses was acquired for two seriously wounded men and another man was pushed along in a wheelbarrow ... They marched for six hours and at half past six in the morning of 29 May they reached Bambecque. [a couple of kilometres north of Herzeele]

Why they were not discovered beggars belief but the plan seems to have succeeded by virtue of its sheer audacity. A gap was found in the German lines and they went through it. The column reached Herzeele at 5.30am and

(*Left*) Captain Leslie Hautin was the Adjutant of the 5/Gloucesters. (*Right*) The compass that was used by Hautin to keep the battalion on course during the breakout on 29 May.

after a short pause moved on to Bambecque, which was reached an hour later. It had been a march reminiscent of that led by Lieutenant Colonel Eric Stephenson of the 2/Dorsets, when fifteen officers and 230 men broke out from a surrounded Festubert on 28 May and marched 10 miles across country to Estaires.

Bill Haywood, the 8/Worcesters Adjutant, wrote of his joy at seeing the Gloucesters arrive at Bambecque, a battalion he was sure had been overwhelmed:

> During the early morning stand-to I saw a wonderful sight. Round the corner as I came out of Battalion Headquarters appeared the survivors of the 5th Gloucesters. They were dirty, weary and haggard, but unbeaten. Their eyes were sunken and red from lack of sleep, and their feet as they marched seemed to me no more than an inch from the ground ... for a second I just stared, then I recognized the burly Colonel Buxton stumbling along at the head of his men. Behind him was Hauting, the Adjutant, with two prisoners. I spotted Major Mason and young Shephard with his head bandaged. I ran forward and Colonel Buxton almost tottered into my arms. I said, 'You are hurt sir', he mumbled, 'I'm peppered all over Bill. None of it serious.' Major Priestly, the second in command, came forward, and I suggested he should rest the troops a few minutes.

Buxton's men had one more journey to make; orders came through from brigade that the Gloucesters were to travel by road to Rexpoëde where they took up their last positions of the campaign before marching to Bray Dunes. There they met up with Major Priestly, the RSM and thirty men who had become separated from the battalion at Rexpoëde and eventually embarked for England.

Chapter 5

Wormhout

26–28 May 1940

The greater part of the 2/Royal Warwicks arrived in Wormhout in the pouring rain just before dawn on 26 May, where they halted in the town square to await orders from the commanding officer, Major Phillip Hicks. The Battalion Medical Officer, Captain Tony Crook, remembered going to sleep on the pavement with his tin hat still on his head and having a 'marvellous kip' despite the rain. Hicks had been in Wormhout since their orders had come through from brigade at midnight the previous day and by 7.00am companies were in position and Battalion Headquarters was established at Château Morael, a large building situated at the junction of Rue d'Esquelbecq with the village square, and shared with 42-year-old Major James Rance, commanding Headquarters Company. It was also home to the headquarters of 53/Anti-Tank Regiment. The regimental aid post was opened in a house to the rear of Château Morael by Captain Crook:

> I was allocated another large house with reasonable cellars and a decent exit onto the Wormhout-Dunkirk road, so we were busy getting ourselves sorted and making certain the company stretcher bearers knew where we were ... The family who lived in our RAP

Some of the Royal Warwicks officers taken in January 1940. Left to right: Captain Hyde, Captain Tomes, the French interpreter, Lieutenant Colonel Dunn, Captain Nicholson, Major Hicks, Lieutenant Gunnell and Captain Crook RAMC.

house had determined to stick it out, as their son was an invalid in a wheelchair. I visited them again nearly fifteen years later and they were still there and the invalid still in his wheelchair. They said the kit and clothes we left behind after we had been captured were invaluable to them all through the war.

Company Positions

The Warwicks were responsible for the defence of the western side of the town and Hicks, during his visits to each company, made it clear to all that their position at Wormhout was to be held until the last round. Having lost C Company (Captain Charles Nicholson) from the outlying village of Esquelbecq, Hicks seemed happy enough with B Company and 37-year-old Captain Edward Jerram on the right, covering the D17 Esquelbecq road and the north western and western approaches, with Second Lieutenant Basil Gunnell's 10 Platoon north of the road and Lieutenant Charles Dunwell straddling it. Major Cecil Chichester-Constable and A Company were in the centre and D Company, under Captain Frazer Lynn-Allen, was holding the line of the D55 Ledringhem road to the road from Cassel. Each company had a frontage of about 800 yards and company strengths averaged eighty to ninety men in each. The 8/Worcesters were responsible for the eastern half of the town, which included the D55 to Wylder, where Brigadier Hamilton's Brigade Headquarters was situated. Within the semi-circle occupied by the 2/Warwicks on the western side of town, the anti-tank guns of 53/Anti-Tank Regiment and the machine guns of the 4/Cheshires supported the infantry.

Captain Edward Jerram.

27 May

Although the general situation did not appear to be idyllic, the night of 26 May was passed in relative quiet despite the heavy rain. The peace of the morning was disturbed by convoys of troops, both British and French, moving through the town on their way to Dunkerque. Several paused to jettison equipment and vehicles, stating that they had been told to proceed to the coast on foot. The disquiet that these convoys created was added to by the squadrons of German aircraft that continually flew overhead on their way to bomb Dunkerque, where a thick pall of smoke was visible from the top storey of the RAP. The situation was obviously considerably

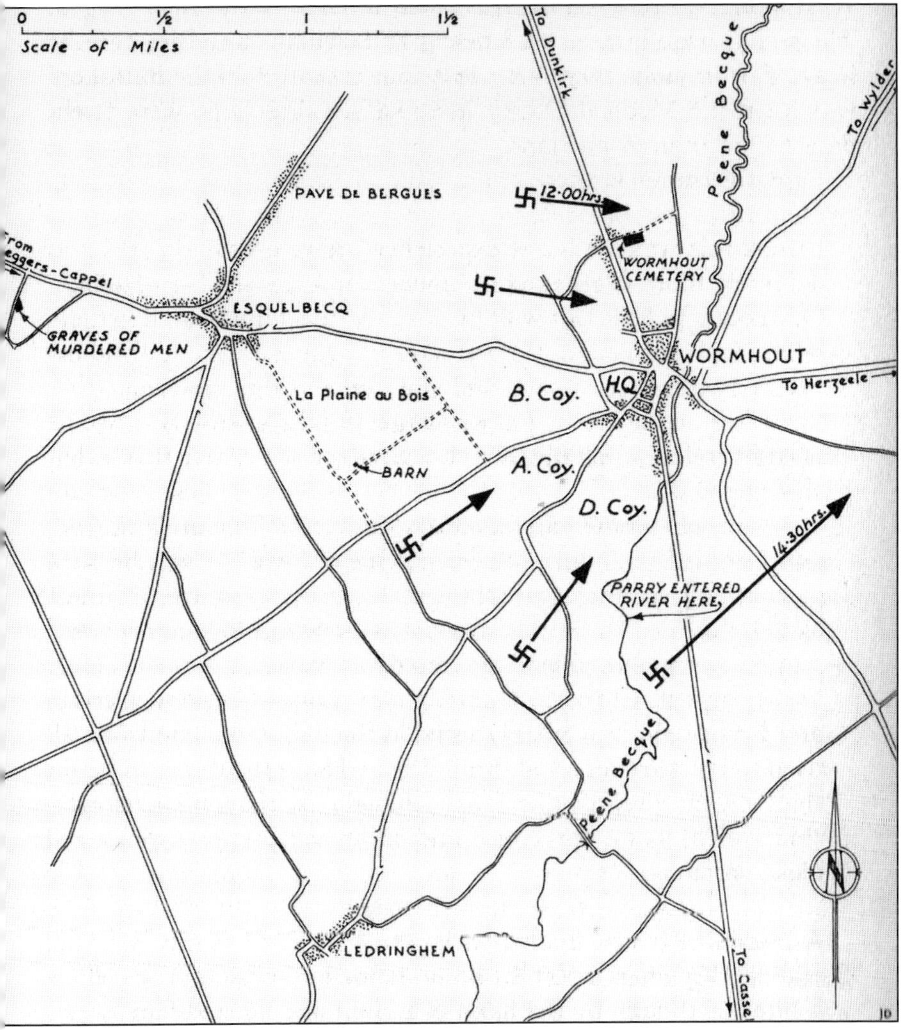

A slightly inaccurate map of the Warwicks' positions at Wormhout. The position of B Company should indicate they were also deployed to the north, across the Esquelbecq road.

worse than they had expected, leaving Captain Dick Tomes, the Battalion Adjutant, to confide in his diary:

> But in the back of our minds was the knowledge that there was little chance for most of us ever to get back. We were so tired out from our incessant night moves, lack of sleep and complicated withdrawals, that our brains could not grasp the full significance of everything.

In the afternoon of 27 May Wormhout was bombed by fifteen to twenty Stukas, who came in low, and took their time over the raid. Light anti-

Wormhout was bombed by fifteen to twenty Stukas on 27 May.

aircraft fire from the battalion's Bren guns was almost totally ineffectual and Dick Tomes felt the raid was one of the worst experiences he had had:

> One felt sickened and exhausted with the clamour and violence and the knowledge that there were none of our own planes to take on the enemy bombers. I tried to collect some men for concerted small arms fire, but this was hopeless.

Captain Tony Crook was horrified to watch the civilian houses crumble into dust and was kept busy by the number of civilian casualties who came into the battalion RAP. Thankfully, there was still a French first aid post in the town and the majority of the civilian casualties were tended to there. To everyone's relief, Battalion Headquarters was not hit but the town was a shambles, every house was either wrecked completely or partially and the square was a mass of debris. Fallen trees, telegraph wires and smashed civilian vans were everywhere and two bombs exploded in the nearby park, wounding six men of the Pioneer Platoon and smashing several military vehicles. Once the air raid had finished and the last aircraft had departed, Battalion Headquarters was moved out of Château Morael and into slit trenches at the far end of the park.

28 May

The bombing was an early indication that the town was about to be attacked and, having passed a reasonably quiet night on the 27th, enemy reconnaissance groups were spotted the next morning on the right flank.

The battalion Regimental Aid Post on the D916.

After the air raid on 27 May Château Morael was abandoned.

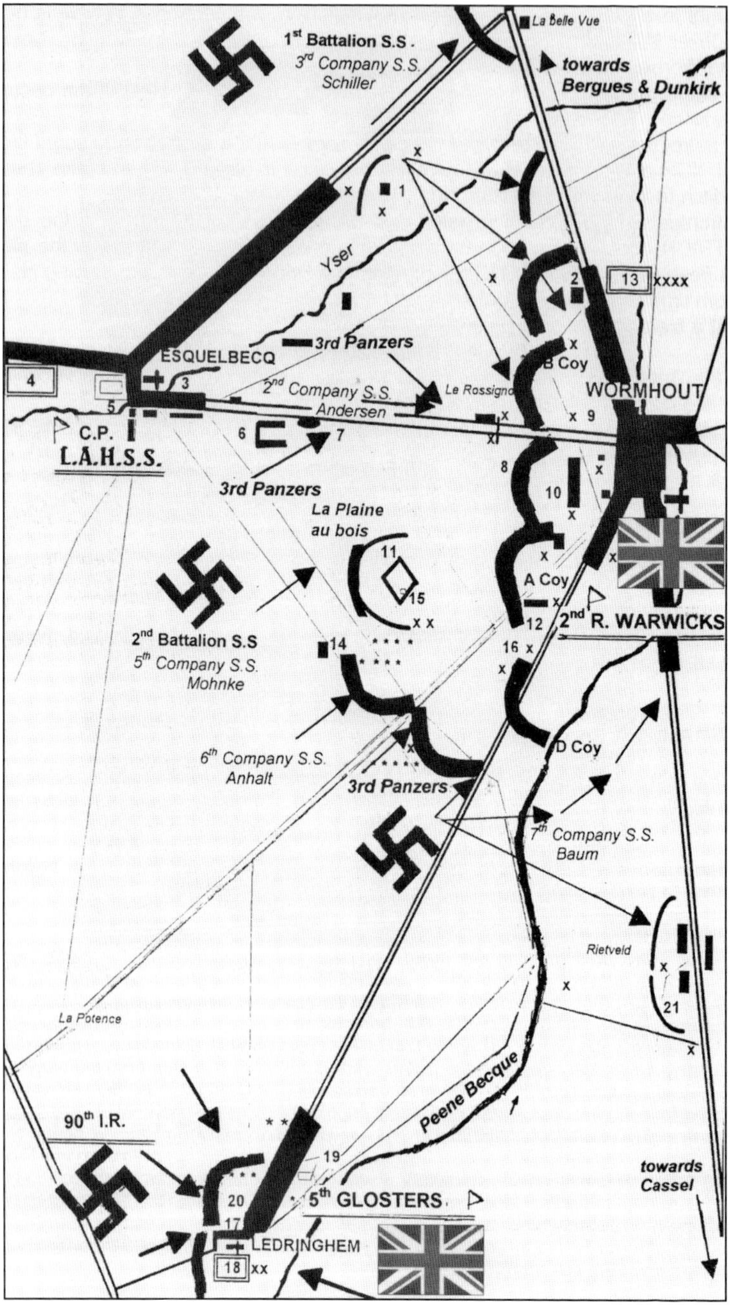

A map taken from Guy Rommelaere's book, showing the attack of 28 May on Wormhout and Ledringhem.

Captain Edward Jerram was having breakfast with Second Lieutenant Gunnell in a slit trench when they heard shots being fired from the Esquelbecq road. Gunnell was immediately ordered to investigate and found a German patrol had been stopped at the barricade and turned around amidst a fusillade of shots from the Cheshire machine gunners. Jerram's diary records the battle beginning from the direction of Esquelbecq at 9.40am but other sources suggest 7.45am.

What they did not know was the attacking force was made up of SS troops and vehicles. Apparently, Captain Jerram's B Company were dealing with a mass of refugees heading towards Wormhout who had been halted at the roadblock. Suddenly, several German vehicles appeared and were immediately shot up by fire from an anti-tank gun and burst into flames. In the confusion that followed 'the Boche jumped out into the fields on either side' and entered the adjacent building from where they machine gunned the roadblock. These were either men of the 2/Battalion LSAH, commanded by *Sturmbannführer* Ernst Schützeck, who had been allocated the town of Wormhout as the main focus of their attack; or men of *Obersturmbannführer* Martin Kohlröser's 1/Battalion LSAH, en route to attack the northern sector of the town. Whichever battalion they came from, it was a nasty shock for a regiment that so far had had a relatively easy campaign.

A German map showing the attack on Wormhout on 28 May.

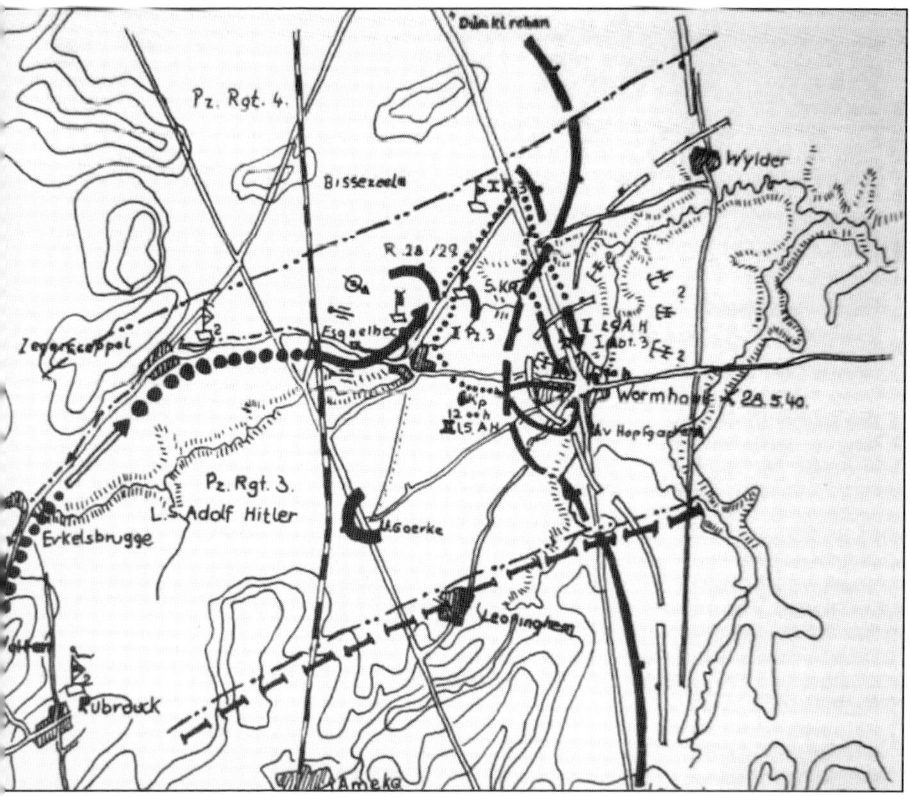

Château Bergerot, Esquelbecq.

At 8.00am forty-two German tanks from the 2nd Panzer Division had entered Esquelbecq unopposed and Sepp Dietrich's men established their advanced Regimental Headquarters in the 13th century Château Bergerot. *Leutnant* von Hopfgarten, a Wehrmacht officer, was commanding 5/*Kompanie* of the 3/Panzer Regiment:

> *Oberleutnant* Kapferer outlined to us the situation. 'The enemy is defending fiercely the last sticking point: Wormhout. The 2/Panzer Regiment is standing by to join in and to that end is moving to the edge of Esquelbecq' ... Towards 9.00am we reached the edge of Esquelbecq ourselves, numerous meadows, surrounded by hedges, higher than a man, afforded us good opportunities to hide. Wormhout lay about 800m ahead of us. We expected every moment the order to attack, but waiting was the order of the day.

If Dietrich felt the *Leibstandarte* would be able to overwhelm the Warwicks without tank support, his apparent confidence did not support the facts confronting him, as all three companies of Warwicks held their positions until around noon.

Dietrich's Humiliation

At this point in the battle there was an incident which very possibly had an impact on what took place later in the day. Becoming impatient with the apparent lack of success by Schützeck's 2/Battalion LSAH in overpowering the Warwicks, Dietrich ordered up a Mercedes cross country vehicle and, along with the adjutant of the 15/Motorcycle Company, *Obersturmführer* Max Wünche, he set off from Esquelbecq in a convoy of vehicles to discover what had brought the 2/Battalion LSAH to a halt. At 11.50am Dietrich's Mercedes was abruptly stopped by a barrage of fire from 8 Platoon of the Cheshires under the command of Lieutenant Geoffrey Clemence, positioned between the le Rossignol and Bollengier farms. Max Wünche gives this account of the episode:

> While we were driving along we could not hear the detonations of the battle, and our vigilance was relaxed. A roadblock obstructing the road brought us to a halt. As we got out to clear our path and move the obstruction, we came under heavy fire.

The command vehicle was hit and burst into flames and the driver killed outright. Dietrich and Wünche just had enough time to take cover in a ditch, lying prone and not daring to raise their heads. Wünche continues the account:

> Fortunately the ditch was fairly deep, as the bullets were ricocheting non-stop from the verges. We tried to withdraw backwards, but it was impossible because the entrance to a field cut across the ditch and we should have to pass through the drainage pipe. During this time our

Sepp Dietrich's Mercedes after it had been hit by the Cheshire machine gunners.

car continued to blaze and petrol began to run out of the fuel tank. I was attempting to get into the drain but could only get partway because it was blocked up. I later lost consciousness and do not recall what happened afterwards.'

The two men had to remain in the ditch until 3.00pm, during which time the regiment thought Dietrich was dead. He resorted to covering himself with slurry from the Bollengier pigsties in order not to be burnt alive by the petrol. All this on his forty-eighth birthday! Meanwhile, *Sturmbannführer* Ernst Schützeck had been badly wounded in the market place at Wormhout and was found by Hermann Hasenwinkle lying in his vehicle, apparently close to death. Command of the battalion fell to *Hauptsturmführer* Wilhelm Mohnke.

Initial efforts to extract Dietrich and Wünche from the ditch were in vain; the 2/Battalion LSAH attempted to free its commander but was prevented from doing so by heavy machine gun fire. A reinforced platoon from 6/ *Kompanie* of the 2nd Panzer Brigade, under *Leutnant* Corder, also tried to reach the two men but lost four tanks in the attempt to the guns of 53/Anti-Tank Regiment and Corder, together with his second in command, *Feldwebel* Cramell, were killed. By the afternoon the 1/Battalion LSAH had managed to fight its way into the south western sector of Wormhout by travelling north of Esquelbecq and, with this new threat facing the men of B Company, the pressure was diverted from Dietrich's predicament and a patrol from the 1/Battalion LSAH led by *Hauptsturmführer* Ernst Meyer

***Obersturmführer* Max Wünche.**

***Hauptsturmführer* Ernst Meyer.**

completed the successful recovery of the regimental commander in an action he details in his autobiography:

> The commander was finally freed from his predicament by an assault team from the 1/Leibstandarte, commanded by *Hauptsturnführer* Ernst Meyer. Unfortunately the leader of the assault troops, the courageous *Oberscharfuhrer* Oberschelp, was killed. Oberschelp was the first non-commissioned officer of the regiment to receive the Iron Cross First Class during the Polish campaign.

Midday on 28 May

By mid morning, Dick Tomes recorded only three or four men killed and some fourteen others wounded. Although the British positions were largely intact, substantial enemy activity in the form of shell and mortar fire changed the course of the battle, heralded by their old friend the reconnaissance aircraft with the bogus French markings:

> With no opposition it flew backwards and forwards, observing and spotting and we were powerless to stop it. Shortly afterwards, owing to this, the shelling became more intense and deadly. This plane was able to direct mortar fire extremely accurately onto slit trenches and anti-tank guns, causing large casualties in men and guns before the actual attack came.

It was the inability to free their regimental commander from the ditch on the Esquelbecq road that may well have led to the tanks being summoned, ostensibly to free Dietrich, but in reality to bring a new momentum to the attack that was in great danger of stalling in the face of British opposition. Little detail is known of the German attack on the three companies of Warwickshires at Wormhout, except that of B Company, which is covered in Jerram's diary account. Corporal William 'Bill' Cordrey of B Company was south of the Esquelbecq road in slit trenches when the tanks headed off towards the south west of the town. He was armed with a Boys anti-tank rifle and described the action at the height of the battle:

> The tanks were facing us 700 yards away, lined up and advancing relentlessly. I was ordering our men to take cover. We received more than a dozen salvos! What an inferno! Everyone was firing now and I had my sights on the centre tank. I couldn't miss. I was giving it the whole round, and although I knew it was a bull's eye the tank kept coming as if nothing had happened. What a joke, the bloody tank never faltered, and I knew I was hitting it.

The tanks kept on advancing and it looked very much as if they would be overrun:

> At the very moment for withdrawing, Clancey suddenly shouted: 'Look, they're turning!' I looked and saw the whole line of advancing

tanks veering left, the right hand tank was going to miss us by a hundred yards! I couldn't believe my eyes. A few minutes more and they would have flattened us.

Cordrey and his section were spared but others, such as the section on his right, were not so fortunate. Lieutenant Charles Dunwell and A Section were wiped out, while 32-year-old Lance Corporal Walter Handyside of 11 Platoon found himself alone, firing his Bren gun. Jerram writes that Handyside then turned up near Battalion Headquarters with a 'bleeding forehead and a jammed Bren gun', explaining that he was the only one left in his section and that the others had disappeared to the west. Instructing Handyside to gather all the men he could and take them back up to the front line, it was the last he saw of an 'exceedingly gallant and brave man'. Handyside was killed some time later. Corporal Thomas later told Cordrey that a tank had driven right over his trench, killing everyone except himself but crushing his legs.

Corporal William Cordrey.

After Cordrey had withdrawn to Company Headquarters he came across 39-year-old Platoon Sergeant Major (PSM) Charles Agutter in need of urgent medical attention. Commandeering a vehicle, Cordrey, Clancey and two other men, headed off in search of the RAP. On entering Wormhout they found the town ablaze and decided to drive towards Dunkerque but as they were leaving the town they were halted by a road block. Returning to the burning town amidst a hail of gunfire the vehicle finally came to a halt after falling into a bomb crater. PSM Agutter was now dead and Cordrey's party was surrounded by German infantry:

> We got out, threatened by an SS [soldier], who spoke little English. My feet hadn't even touched the ground before another soldier jammed a revolver against my stomach and raved at me in German. I could feel the huge tension gripping the SS around us but that took the biscuit. I could feel the revolver trembling, and just waited for the final bullet. Suddenly he turned away, issuing orders, and thirty of so SS took us back where we had come from.

Fleeting accounts of the attack on Wormhout are mentioned by survivors of the massacre in their statements to the Judge Advocate's Office and more information can be gleaned from the battalion's missing men files.

D Company

Sergeant Homer of D Company remembers his headquarters was positioned in a 'very thick wood' where they were bombed repeatedly by enemy aircraft. Tanks appeared in the afternoon and Homer writes that he thought the company was surrounded. After they had been pushed back, he came across Captain Lynn-Allen treating four badly wounded men. From there Homer was sent to Brigade Headquarters with a message from Captain Lynn-Allen. Passing through German occupied territory he eventually arrived at Brigade Headquarters and was ordered to stay put by Dennis Gibbs, the Brigade Major. That message probably saved his life.

D Company is also mentioned by 19-year-old Private Albert 'Bert' Evans in his testimony. He remembers a heavy mortar attack and tanks that fanned out, allowing him to see the infantrymen following up behind. Running to the rear of his position, he was confronted by the waters of the Peene Becque and while others jumped into the water, Evans, being unable to swim, was captured.

A Company

A similar story was evident in the A Company area, but even before it became apparent that the company positions had been overwhelmed, Private Reginald West, a Headquarters Company signaller, was asked to send a message to the company commander, Major Chichester-Constable, a man who had already won the Military Cross in the First World War. Realizing that the line was dead, he and 22-year-old Lieutenant David Padfield set off towards Fort Rose Farm with a reel of cable but were met by German tanks accompanied by SS infantry. Escape was out of the question but, to West's amazement, Padfield's reaction was to pull out his pistol, either in surrender or defiance, an action which led to his immediate death. West was overpowered and taken prisoner. Some time before, Major Chichester-Constable was seen walking towards the approaching enemy tanks with pistol in hand. We are told he died in the arms of an SS soldier, who himself was killed the next day.

Private Reginald West was with David Padfield when he was killed.

The 4/Cheshires

As with 8 Platoon of the Cheshires, situated on or near to the Esquelbecq road, the remaining platoons were spread amongst the Warwickshire infantry companies. 15 Platoon, under Second Lieutenant Ravenscroft, was in the centre, which gives them an approximate location somewhere in the A Company positions. At about 1.30pm they took up a fresh position in the town, one section firing down the Cassel road and a second firing up the Dunkerque road. According to the account of Lance Corporal Thomas Oxley, who was in the second section, a German attack must have managed a breakthrough as they unexpectedly stumbled across German infantry when they entered the town square:

> We drove into the centre of Wormhout square; just as we went round the corner by the church we were amazed to see a large party of Germans at the other end. I observed the time on the church clock and it was 1.50pm. They appeared to be resting but immediately they observed us they opened fire. Most of the men in our two trucks were either killed or wounded. My truck gave a sudden turn and I was thrown off, and the truck went on ... The Germans immediately crowded round us, shouting and storming and pointing their weapons at us ... After a matter of minutes they fired on us. Whether they all fired I cannot say, but definitely one of them who I had been watching let go a burst on his Tommy gun at the four of us. I was hit twice in the arm and leg.

Oxley was knocked out immediately. When he regained consciousness he had the presence of mind to remain perfectly still, just watching his captors. While doing so three soldiers brought out an English sergeant. He appeared to be badly wounded and a German officer immediately shot him with his revolver. As Oxley said afterwards, 'he emptied his revolver into the sergeant whilst he lay on the ground'.

Heavy mortar fire prompted the timely departure of the Germans at 4.50pm, leaving Oxley to catch the attention of a wounded soldier coming out of a building, who he says had been hiding in a wardrobe. Together they escaped across the fields to the north and were eventually evacuated from the beaches around Dunkerque. Ravenscroft was later wounded in the leg and taken prisoner.

To the left of Ravenscroft's platoon was 13 Platoon, under the command of 24-year-old Lieutenant Basil Glasspool. The platoon was the most southerly of the Cheshire platoons and deployed in two sections and held up the enemy for some time prior to being overrun. Glasspool was last seen leading some of his men towards Wormhout. However, there is some debate over the circumstances of his death. The evidence given by Private Bert Evans of D Company after his capture indicates that at least one section of Glasspool's platoon were taken prisoner and lined up against a shed to the south of Wormhout:

> After a short time we were halted in front of a shed, where there were other prisoners lined up. I could not recognize any of them. They might have been from the Cheshire Regiment. Anyway, there were

SS motorcycle soldiers.

> about fifteen of them, and as they stood there the guards who were in charge of them opened up with automatic fire. They killed the lot. I shall never forget seeing them fall down just like rag dolls. I never understood why, at that moment, we ourselves were spared.

Whether Glasspool was amongst this group is unknown but it would seem probable that he was among the men who were shot down in cold blood, possibly in the manner described by Evans. However, apart from their burial at Ledringhem Churchyard, where Glasspool is buried along with a number of his men, there is little evidence to suggest the men seen by Evans were in fact from Glasspool's platoon. On the other hand, Ledringhem is several miles to the south of Wormhout and much closer to Glasspool's last known position. If he had been executed with his men then his burial in Ledringhem Churchyard would appear to support this. The remaining men of 13 Platoon, according to Major Kissack, were taken to the barn on La Plaine au Bois.

As the German infantry gradually encircled the Warwicks, Tomes wrote of the desperation they faced with German armoured vehicles bursting through their defences:

> The shelling increased, a smoke screen was laid and all the Coys [companies] reported tanks, either attacking or preparing to do so, with infantry behind them. We had no tank obstacles and most of the

25mm and 2-pounder anti-tank guns had been destroyed and their crews killed after their fire had been cleverly drawn. It became obvious that we could not stop a tank attack and would be merely overrun.

53/Anti-Tank Regiment

Tomes' remarks about the anti tank crews being killed were correct. Gunner Jack Creed had been in the 53/Anti Tank Regiment since he had joined 210/Battery in Birmingham during the rush to war in 1937. At Wormhout his gun was near the cemetery to the north of the town, which no doubt contributed to him making his escape:

> Our gun was not in a very good position. We positioned it near a café so that it pointed down a road, and even though we did the best we could in the time allowed, it was still very visible. Tom Nichols and his gun crew were much luckier however, their gun was in a back garden just over the road from us ... The next morning, none of us realized just how serious was our position, for by now we in the town had been almost completely surrounded by the Germans from what I now know to be the 2nd Panzer Division and the infantry of SS Liebstandarte Regiment.

Creed writes that the early part of the morning was quiet apart from one or two French soldiers wandering about aimlessly wearing, what he thought, were old fashioned uniforms. Overhead he noticed a German spotter aircraft but his gun did not fire at it, saving the ammunition for later:

> Sergeant Whistle, who was my troop commander, paid a visit to the café near us and emerged with a number of bottles of champagne ... suddenly thing started to happen. A French policeman began to cross the road to the café and was shot. Now the German mortars began to lob their bombs towards us and these landed increasingly near as time went on ... About 200 yards away down the road a tank fired one shell and some infantry were seen to cross the road.

Taking aim at the tank, the gun jammed at the crucial moment and the gun crew resorted to Bren gun fire. Now totally on their own and without an officer to direct them, no wireless communication or a handy vehicle to escape in, they ran to the rear of the café.

> An infantryman said a possible way out lay through the cemetery some 50 yards or so to our rear. The decision to try it was made in seconds. Two or three of us got to our feet and ran back, first through the cemetery and then into the fields beyond it. At any moment we expected to be shot by the Germans.

Gunner Tom Nichols writes that he did not abandon his weapon until 5.30pm, which does correspond with some of the other evidence from Wormhout. His account states that he and his crew (Gunners Marsh,

The *Liebstandarte* in 1938. Adolf Hitler is pictured on the left, taking the salute.

Matthews and Williams) took a vehicle and headed towards town, in the opposite direction to Creed:

> The Germans stopped firing, perhaps because they thought we were some of their own men. As we drew level I threw a grenade. I cannot have got them all because the firing followed us, killing Private (Edward) Marsh. Wormhout was full of Germans but we escaped by a miracle. My prayer was answered, because suddenly it came onto rain in torrents and the enemy had taken shelter and did not fire on us. The enormous number of dead I saw as we crossed the town was unbelievable; in particular I saw a number of corpses who were entirely naked, covered with, what looked like, sabre cuts and four vehicles full of bodies.

There is no further mention of the state of the bodies or if they were German or British, but it does leave a large question mark as to why they were naked, was this further evidence of a massacre? The report of heavy rain was quite correct, the weather reports for the day indicated several heavy showers and both German and British accounts refer to these downpours. 20-year-old Gunner Marsh is remembered on the Dunkirk Memorial. Creed, and presumably Nichols, eventually met Major Wiggin, the battery commander, who accompanied them to Bray Dunes. Of the original 540 officers and men, only 348 were evacuated from Dunkerque; the remainder were either killed, captured or missing, their anti-tank guns forming a very small part of the equipment left behind in France.

Battalion Headquarters

Back in Wormhout, Tomes' diary recorded the last stand of Battalion Headquarters. They were aware that the Germans had broken through the company positions and Tomes, armed with a Lee Enfield rifle, made his way with a 'man with an anti-tank rifle' towards a couple of armoured cars that were firing from behind a hedge some 200 yards from his position:

> I fired two of the remaining three rounds. I couldn't see whether they had any effect ... After placing the man with the anti-tank rifle in position I fired off practically the whole bandolier [of small arms ammunition] at the crews in the turrets of the armoured cars – one became ditched – and at various vehicles and motor cycles coming along the road ... Then I heard Hicks shouting at me to come back. I saw two tanks coming towards us across the field. They must have wiped out the intelligence section, who were at that corner.

Tomes never made it; he felt a savage blow to his head while trying to climb over a fence and found himself at the Battalion RAP. Captain Tony Crook remembered Tomes arriving:

> At about 4.30pm the adjutant was brought in unconscious with a head wound. When he recovered consciousness he told us that Battalion HQ had departed, that all communications with companies and brigade had been cut and that Germans troops and tanks were all around us ... At about 6.30pm I went up to the top of our house but couldn't see very much except fires. Someone told me that Major Harborne and several others were in a neighbouring house and

A Boys anti-tank rifle, similar to the one that was used during the Warwicks' last stand at Wormhout. Against the relatively thick armour of the German tanks it was next to useless.

> wounded, so I decided to go out and see for myself ... I had hardly gone a hundred yards before a German stormtrooper appeared from behind a bush and covered me with his sub-machine gun, a most unpleasant and frightening moment.

Crook managed to convince the soldier that he was a doctor and was ordered to return to the Royal Warwicks' RAP with the German soldier pointing his gun menacingly at him. Harborne was eventually rescued from the house and taken prisoner but 42-year-old Major James Rance was killed leading a party of men towards the Esquelbecq road. The defence of Wormhout was over.

Of the others, Hicks managed to escape along with Second Lieutenant Tomes (no relation) and sixty-five men, reaching Brigade Headquarters, where they were joined by Second Lieutenant John Vaudrey, the Battalion Intelligence Officer, with another eighteen men, along with Captain Sir John Nicholson, 4/Cheshires. Later Captain Jerram arrived with six men, having had to fight their way across an enemy held bridge. At Brigade Headquarters Hamilton was able to inform Hicks of his promotion to lieutenant colonel! The battalion had certainly delayed the enemy, to the extent that no further advance was made from the town that day, indeed at 8.00pm that evening the Germans withdrew from Wormhout in expectation of a British artillery bombardment.

Chapter 6

The Wormhout Massacres

28 May

There is little doubt that individual acts of barbarism involving both military and civilians did take place around and in Wormhout on 28 May 1940, to some of which attention has already been drawn in Chapter 5. It is also beyond reasonable doubt that these acts were carried out largely by men of the 2/Battalion LSAH, perhaps in retaliation for the episodes involving *Sturmbannführer* Ernst Schützeck and *Gruppenführer* Sepp Dietrich.

What we do know is that a group of men were rounded up and marched to a place opposite the Café St Hubert by Wormhout church. After being stripped of all their personal property they were then marched along Rue de Rubrouck to the farm at Fort Rose, which had been the headquarters of the 2/Battalion LSAH since noon. Here it is said a senior SS officer, possibly *Hauptsturmbanführer* Wilhelm Mohnke, shouted at 28-year-old *Untersturmführer* Heinrichs, rebuking him for taking prisoners. After a short interval the group was double marched across the fields to La Plaine au Bois, where they were herded into a barn and murdered.

A Company

But, before we look in detail at these murders, let us turn to the demise of A Company. Captain Crook writes that he and the surviving members of the RAP were marched out of Wormhout down a small country lane, passing a lot of bodies belonging to A Company. What he says next is quite chilling:

> In retrospect I think I was looking at another massacre; the dead were all lying with their feet in the ditch and their bodies on the verge. It all looked too tidy. It is probable that they had been captured, ordered to line up in the ditch and shot down or, in other words, executed. I was allowed a quick look and found Major Chichester-Constable's body and alongside him Captain David Padfield, another good friend of mine.

There is no hard evidence to support Crook's assertions, whilst separate reports concerning the death of Chichester-Constable and David Padfield suggest that at least one of them may have been killed in the general fighting. However, the manner in which the remainder of the men died is unknown, they were in the area assaulted by the 2/Battalion LSAH and possibly came under the jurisdiction of the 5th and 7th *Kompanies*.

Gunner Alf Davies.

Whether the men were killed before or after surrender will forever remain a mystery.

During this time the D916 was being used by several parties of the BEF to reach Dunkerque, a number of whom fell into German hands as they sought to circumvent the blocked roads east of Wormhout. Gunner Richard Parry of 242/Battery, 69/Medium Regiment, was one of these men. Gunner Alf Davies remembers three vehicles containing about fifty men were ambushed, he and two others managing to escape through the back of a building and later found out that they were the only survivors of the attack who returned home via Dunkerque.

Alf survived the war and died in 2018. Of the others, some eighteen men, including Captain the Earl of Aylesbury, were killed. The survivors appear to have been taken to the barn on La Plaine au Bois, a number which included 19-year-old Bombardier Frank Thompson. It is possible that 19-year-old Lance Bombardier John Coleman and Gunner Ronald Ashley were with him in the barn, as all three men are buried in Wormhoudt Communal Cemetery and remembered on the Llandudno War Memorial. Gunner Parry was one of the men who found refuge in a building near the Peene Becque. Being a strong swimmer, he slipped into the river and swam upstream towards what he later realised was Wormhout. Captured in the town by the SS, he joined the prisoners at Café Hubert near the church. Another group was from 20/Anti-Tank Regiment, a unit from the 3rd Division, which was commanded by Major General Bernard Montgomery. The captured men included Driver John Borland and Gunner 'Nobby' Clarke. Captured by the SS, these men and three others were eventually to end up in the barn on La Plaine au Bois.

A rather poor photograph of the barn on La Plaine au Bois where the massacre took place. The photograph was probably taken after the war.

Interrogation

When the fighting ended, prisoners were collected together and some were interrogated by an officer wearing a monocle. There is no indication as to who this officer might have been or indeed where it took place, but Private Charles Daley of A Company, who had been shot in the shoulder by an SS soldier after surrendering, recognized him as an officer of the LSAH. The largest group of prisoners was from D Company who were overwhelmed by the tank attack west of the Peene Becque and it was this group that Private Bert Evans joined. Here there is some discrepancy between Guy Rommalaere's account and that of Evans. Bert Evans is adamant that after marching across the stream over a wooden bridge, they passed a pillbox and one 'of our chaps who was still at large' threw a grenade into the open turret of a German tank. Rommelaere does not mention this incident and incorrectly places the shooting of the 'fifteen or so' Cheshires at a canning factory near Café Hubert.

Evans certainly found himself near the Café Hubert, where he was joined by a wet and bedraggled Richard Parry, who estimates that they were required to hold up their arms for some fifteen minutes until a German officer appeared and gave them permission to rest. Within this group was

The Bridge over the Peene Becque – a modern replacement.

Private Bert Evans in later life.

also Captain Frazer Lynn-Allen, commanding D Company, a man whose cousin, Captain Esmond Lynn-Allen, was commanding C Company of the 2/Gloucesters at Cassel, a few miles to the south. Moving on again, the party were marched along Rue de Rubrouck and halted at Fort Rose Farm, where they were joined by a party of thirty or forty prisoners, mostly from A Company but evidently including some Cheshires and several gunners. It is possible that Reginald West, the signaler that witnessed David Padfield's death, joined them here.

The time was about 4.30pm and it was then that a senior German officer, 'with a large nose and wearing a soft peaked cap', appeared, 'raving blue murder', giving orders that were understood by one of the British prisoners that the SS

Fort Rose Farm, taken after the war.

were taking no prisoners. It has long been thought that this officer was *Hauptsturmfuhrer* Wilhelm Mohnke, who was now in command of the 2/Battalion LSAH. It may well have been; but it should be said that, although it is likely, there is little evidence that he was the officer in question or that he knew of, or even condoned, the murders that followed, despite Guy Rommelaere's assertions to the contrary.

However, witness testimony by several former SS soldiers, in particular that of *Rottenführer* Oskar Senf, appeared to confirm that the massacre was an order, or the result of an order, given by Mohnke. Unfortunately the 33-year-old Senf died of tuberculosis before the case was brought to trial after the war.

***Hauptsturmführer* Wilhelm Mohnke.**

La Plaine au Bois

After a pause the prisoners were marched across the fields, this time accompanied by a number of soldiers from 8/*Kompanie*, who apparently told *Untersturmführer* Heinrichs that they had been given orders to execute the prisoners, at which point Heinrichs left the group and returned to his company. The exact number of prisoners that were marched across the fields towards the barn at La Plaine au Bois is unclear but once they had all crowded into the barn there were at least a hundred men. The final march of a mile across the fields was harrowing; forced to double march, Charles Daley of A Company found the journey almost unendurable, while Richard Parry and Bert Evans only kept going after seeing other stragglers shot or bayoneted out of hand. Then, just as a shower of rain soaked them again, they saw their destination was the meadow adjacent to a row of trees with a small, open-ended, barn at one end.

Captain Lynn-Allen and Bert Evans

Once the twelve guards had packed the men into the barn they threw stick grenades in amongst the prisoners, Evans was hit in the arm by shrapnel and was standing near Captain Lynn-Allen, the only officer in the barn,

A plan of the massacre site, taken from *The Forgotten Massacre*. 1 and 2 represent the barn, 3 and 4 are where Lynn-Allen and Evans were originally standing in the barn and 5-16 are the approximate positions of the SS guards. 17 is the pond where Lynn-Allen and Evans were shot and 20 is their escape route from the barn

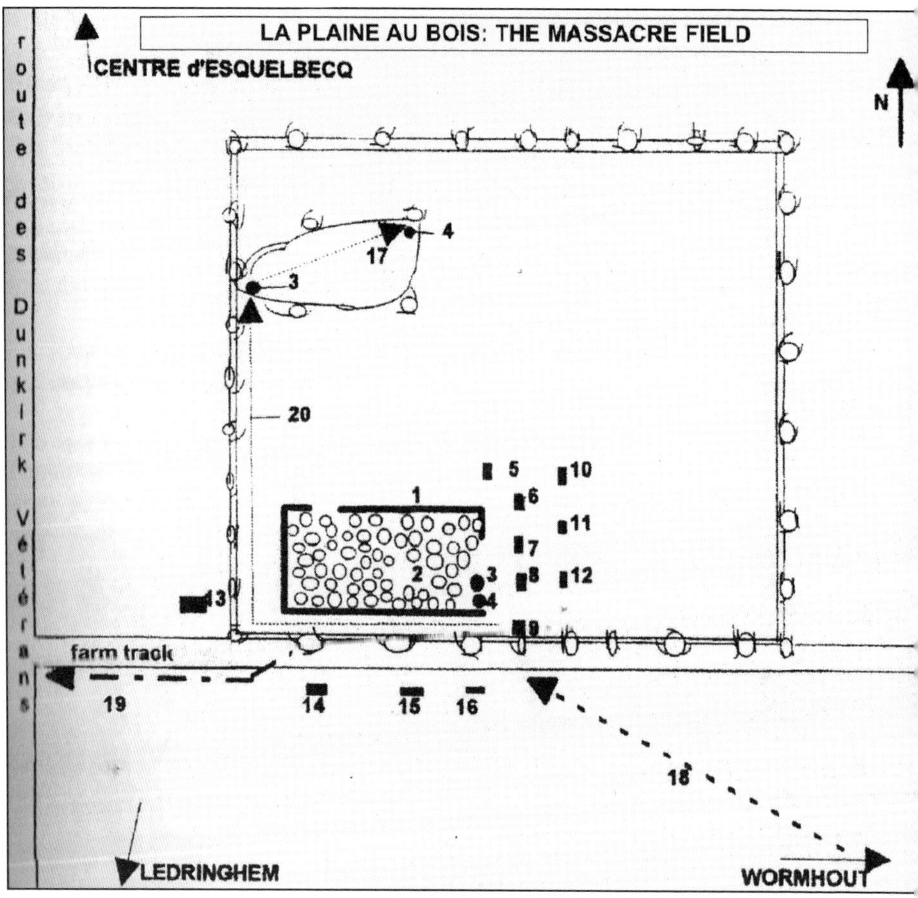

The pond where Captain Lynn-Allen and Bert Evans were shot.

who grabbed him and shouted for him to follow as he ran from the doorway along the line of trees to the pond at the far end. But they were followed. Even submerging themselves in the water was of little use as the guard, thought to be *Scharführer* Walter Drescher, shot Lynn-Allen and Evans, he thought killing both men. Only Evans survived, crawling away to reach a nearby farm, where he was spotted by a Wehrmacht officer:

> When he saw me the officer took hold of me and laid me down on the ground. He made a tourniquet for my arm with a piece of women's clothing. Then he covered me with his raincoat and put me in the back of the motorcycle sidecar. I think he was a doctor.

Evans' arm was amputated but he had been lucky, thanks to the bravery of Captain Lynn-Allen. Evans died in October 2013, the last survivor of the massacre.

Back at the barn, infuriated SS guards continued to throw stick grenades amongst the prisoners, killing Company Sergeant Major Augustus Jennings and Sergeant Stanley Moore, who sacrificed their lives by throwing themselves on top of the exploding grenades, an act which should have resulted in two posthumous Victoria Crosses. Moore and Jennings are buried at Esquelbecq Military Cemetery. Richard Parry counted five or six explosions. The first wounded him in the right leg and threw him outside the wall of the barn. Unable to see inside, he could see everything that was going on outside. Almost in disbelief, he witnessed the SS guards call out five men and execute them. Gunner Brian Fahey from 52/Anti-Tank Regiment was in the second group:

> Then the SS came back to the barn and ordered five more to come out and die. I volunteered because I know we would all have to go through

Captain James Frazer Lynn-Allen.

CSM Augustus Jennings.

> it and it was no use prolonging our last moments of life. I thought at that time that this is what happened when you were taken prisoner; the lad next to me, who was very young, shook my hand and spoke to me, saying, 'I don't know who you are, but I need to shake hands with you' . . . The Nazi NCO lined us up facing his men. There were five of them, each one with a rifle. Facing the executioners, I was number five, and I heard the first four numbers called out, the shot which followed, and my comrades falling, one by one, beside me.

Fahey heard his number being called out and felt the shot pierce his back and pass through his chest. He lost consciousness. When the SS turned him over and saw blood pouring from his nose and mouth they assumed he was dead. It was now close to 5.00pm and killing all the prisoners, five at a time, would take most of the evening; in any case no more British prisoners were prepared to leave the barn unless it was to escape. Conferring briefly, the SS began shooting into the barn indiscriminately; Private Robert Wildsmith, who was probably a member of B Company, recalled the moment that *Rottenführer* Werner Ruger (Ritter in Aitken's account) was hit by his comrades:

> The SS opened fire on us with machine guns; two were firing into the main doorway, two at the side of the barn and one behind. I could see through a hole in the barn wall that the German who was firing behind the barn was hit. Taking advantage of the fact that the Nazis were concerned with their comrade, I escaped across a field by way of a ditch.

While two of the SS carried away the injured Ruger, Charles Daley was hit twice more in his right arm and left leg during this fusillade of shots and, bleeding profusely, he fainted. The nightmare continued, with the SS trampling over the bodies, spraying the prisoners with their machine guns

Those in the barn dived to the ground and attempted to protect themselves as best they could. Richard Parry watched with horror as an SS soldier fired at almost point blank range at him, the bullet passing through his mouth and exiting at the back of his cheek. Parry lost consciousness.

Humphries' Escape

The cries from the wounded and dying men inside the barn were terrible. Private Joseph Humphries of the 4/Cheshires was wounded in the leg and found himself in the centre of the barn beneath a pile of bodies. Lying still until he was sure the SS had gone, he and two others clambered out through an opening in the wall and crawled towards a farmhouse. Humphries' two companions were shot down by a burst of automatic fire, leaving the Cheshire gunner alone and heading towards Cassel. Travelling all the next day across country, he finally met a group of soldiers who turned out to be Cheshires and was taken to the unit's company commander, where he was given a rifle and a steel helmet. The officer may well have been Second Lieutenant Robert Reid of B Company, who was commanding a composite force from B Company and was killed during German mortar fire on 29 May. Humphries was eventually taken prisoner when they were 'surrounded by a squad of Germans using motorbikes and sidecar combinations'.

At the barn it became clear that a number of other men had escaped, although the SS believed they had killed all the prisoners. Private Reginald West remained at large in France for five months before he was recaptured in the south of France. Private George Hopper was one of the few men who remained physically unharmed from his ordeal on the barn but, sadly, on making his way to a nearby farmhouse was recaptured. It was a similar story with Private Alf Tombs, who emerged from the barn with Corporal Gill and Lance Corporal Box, along with Privates Dutton and Cooper. Running into a group of German soldiers, who shot Box dead as they ran across fields, they were eventually handed over to another German army unit. Other escapers were John Borland, 'Nobby' Clarke and three others who managed to open the door in the farthest corner of the barn and run across the fields to safety. These five men were found by the Wehrmacht and taken prisoner the next morning in Rue Vert Vallon.

For those who remained alive in the barn, Charles Daley, Brian Fahey, Richard Parry and others, they clung onto life for two more days until they were found by a Wehrmacht Ambulance Unit and cared for as prisoners of war. It is virtually impossible to say how many men were murdered in the barn or during the forced march across the fields to the Plaine au Bois. The barn itself measured 21 feet by 10 foot 6 inches, enough room for 105 men; Daley thinks there were about ninety while Evans reckons they were between ninety and a hundred men. Thus, with about fifteen known survivors, it would appear that some eighty-five men were murdered.

Gunner Brian Fahey in later life. Fahey freelanced after 1959, working with recording companies, the BBC and the theatre. He provided scores for films and became principal conductor of the BBC Scottish Radio Orchestra in 1972. He was also Shirley Bassey's musical director from 1967 to 1972. He died in 2007.

The Trial

Regrettably, the court case in 1946 against Mohnke and Dietrich proved fruitless. Mohnke was a prisoner of the Russians and Dietrich invoked the SS Oath of Allegiance on the surviving members of the regiment. If there was an individual that bore responsibility for the murders it was Dietrich, a man who claimed that he had been absent from the situation when hiding in the ditch on the Esquelbecq road. He was, however, convicted for his part in the massacres at Malmedy in 1944. His sentence was reduced from twenty-five to ten years; his freedom was short-lived, for he was again arrested for the 1934 executions during the Röhm Purge and died in 1966. Mohnke escaped any retribution that might have been due to him and was released from Russian imprisonment in 1955. He died, at the age of ninety, in 2001. To this date no one individual or individuals have been held to account over the murders.

The Dead

Those that did not survive the massacre in the barn were buried in a mass grave on the Plaine au Bois but, as their identity tags had been removed, many remained unidentified when the grave was exhumed in 1941. Realizing a crime had been committed, it is thought the Germans dispersed the bodies, resulting in the exact location of all the dead being lost. At least six men from D Company, 8/Worcesters, were reportedly in the barn along with several more from the Royal Artillery; but, as their bodies were never found, it is quite possible that many of these victims may either be amongst the unidentified burials at Wormhoudt Communal and Esquelbecq Military

The inauguration of the memorial on the Esquelbecq road on 20 May 1973. Left to right: Bert Evans, John Lavalle, Alf Tombs and Charles Daley.

Cemeteries, or they are perhaps still buried somewhere on the Plaine au Bois. They are remembered on the Dunkirk Memorial. The only Frenchman killed in the massacre was Private Robert Vanpee, who is buried in Esquelbecq Military Cemetery.

The Llandudno connection

Before the Second World War, Llandudno's Drill Hall was home of part-time volunteers of the Territorial Army. In July 1939 it became headquarters to a regular unit, the 69/Medium Regiment (Caernarvon & Denbigh Yeomanry) Royal Artillery. As well as volunteers from the Territorial Army, there was a massive recruitment drive across North Wales in order to reach full strength. The Regiment landed in Le Havre, France, in May 1940, just as the German army swept through the Low Countries and into France. A number of its soldiers died in the Wormhout massacre in 1940.

The 69/Medium Regiment, including Llandudno's 'D' Troop, was mobilized on 1 September 1939, two days before war was declared, under the command of Lieutenant Colonel Clement Arnold. The Regiment landed in Le Havre, France, in May 1940. Llandudno was formally twinned with Wormhout on April 14 1989.

Chapter 7

The 8/Worcesters and Bambecque

26–29 May

On 28 May Bill Haywood took up the appointment of acting Adjutant of the Worcesters, taking over from Captain Vaughn. He remained in the grounds of Château Maes with Lieutenant Colonel James Johnstone. Hamilton had obviously kept the battalion out of the fight in Wormhout, surmising that there was little point in sacrificing Johnstone's men in a battle that would inevitably move north. In this he was again correct, for the Worcesters would face the enemy at Bambecque. However, until the moment when Hamilton decided to withdraw to Rexpoëde, the small group of Worcesters and the men of Brigade Headquarters were preparing to defend the château. Haywood wrote of the mild chaos that followed:

> Everybody remained very cheerful, although it seemed obvious that we should soon be fighting without hope of relief. Jonah (Major S.W. Jones, the Worcester's Second in Command) was seen to smoke his first cigarette for years, and various minor-prophets at once saw calamity! The situation was so critical that Denis Gibbs (the Brigade Major) authorized the destruction of Brigade Headquarters' confidential documents. Carey came forward with the tin box holding these papers, and threw it into the lake, much as the swans protested. To our horror the box sank and then floated to the surface. A signaler raised his rifle and fired a shot or two. Instead the lid flew open and the papers floated on the water, while the hungry swans pounced on them, hoping they would be edible.

Haywood, like many of the officers of 144 Brigade, had a high opinion of Denis Gibbs, although at the time Gibbs was less than popular with Brigadier Hamilton:

> He was tall, almost painfully thin, good-tempered and a first-class soldier. He had a habit of throwing back his head when he laughed, and his busy brown moustache would waggle up and down.

With regard to the papers there is no more reference to them so that we can safely assume they remained out of the clutches of the enemy. The bombs that the Luftwaffe dropped on Wormhout during the afternoon were largely avoided at the château, although one or two caused some concern. The weather, which had been fine all afternoon, suddenly broke and a heavy rainstorm provided Hamilton with the opportunity to move north.

All that is left of the chateau today is the stable block.

Captain Ted Berry was sent into Wormhout with two of his carriers to keep the Germans occupied, which he did by circling around the market square, liberally spraying any German infantry with Bren gun fire until an anti-tank gun scored a direct hit on his kit and ruined a chest of tools. A very disgruntled Berry returned to the château, complaining of the damage to his private property and where, according to Haywood, not even a wet cigarette cheered him up!

Dennis Gibbs in later life.

Captain Ted Berry.

C Company on parade at Bromsgrove in 1938.

Withdrawal

The withdrawal across the fields to the north was underway at 5.00pm. The surviving Warwicks went first, then Brigade and the Worcester's Headquarters Company, along with the survivors of 53/Anti-Tank Regiment under 37-year-old Major Richard Wiggin, leaving the Worcester's C Company to act as rearguard. At Herzeele Major Geoffrey Day and Captain Geoffrey Dorrell had salvaged a fleet of trucks and cars and the battalion drove the last couple of miles into Bambecque.

Bambecque

Once in the village, B Company were quickly deployed in platoon localities, covering the bridge over the Yser and the east of the village in the region of Rue Principale and the C Company platoons scattered themselves around the church in the western half of the village. Headquarters Company were sent on to Rexpoëde to give some protection to the rear. Nearly every house had its shutters down and Battalion Headquarters was opened in an empty shop in the village street. The village may have been deserted but, Haywood noted, there was plenty of evidence of the British having being there:

> To the great delight of our men, we found an abandoned clothing dump near the church. The Colonel and I went to have a look at it and found shelves stacked high with battledresses, shirts, boots and web equipment. Most of our men needed a change. Their uniforms were torn and dirty and their boots sadly worn. This dump was a godsend and the colonel instructed his officers to make full use of it for their men.

Every man must have known that if the battalion was attacked there was little they could do against the might of the panzers and the overwhelming numbers of the LSAH. That they would fight was a foregone conclusion, but for how long? To hold out was a different matter entirely.

29 May

It was during the early morning stand-to that the 5/Gloucesters arrived at Bambecque, an occasion that has already been described in Chapter 4. Sometime after this Johnstone sent Haywood to establish a new Battalion Headquarters at a farm on the Bambecque to Rexpoëde road, a farm he describes as being below the skyline and immediately opposite a park leading to another farm. At the same time the war diary reported that hundreds of French soldiers, on their way to Dunkerque, were passing through Bambecque, a procession that was watched by the Worcesters with a mixture of feelings. Hamilton had already confirmed that there were no hope of any relief and they were to hold on until 9.00pm that night and, with this in mind, Johnston went down to Bambecque to visit B and C Companies, no doubt to give them the good news!

A Company

At about 11.30am the enemy attacked A Company at Wylder from the direction of Wormhout, prompting the 30-year-old John Farrar to withdraw the company to strengthen his force of B Company men at Groenspriet. It remained quiet until 4.00pm, at which point the enemy attacked both companies in overwhelming numbers. An hour later Farrar sent his last message, to the effect that three large and five small tanks were in his area. The silence after that message told the story of their demise. After Farrar had ordered a piecemeal withdrawal, he was last seen firing an anti-tank rifle and was killed on the way back to Bambecque. John Farrar is remembered on the Dunkirk Memorial.

Three officers and sixty other ranks managed to get to Battalion Headquarters, presumably that number included Lieutenant Anslow.

One troop of 210 and 211/Battery, along with three anti-tank guns, under Second Lieutenant Hollis, had been deployed to support Captain Farrar. The 210/Battery War Diary recorded some of the fighting:

> The enemy attacked heavily with infantry and tanks. The tanks mostly came from the rear and unfortunately the guns were sited so they were unable to fire. Buildings were shot down over them and their positions became untenable from machine-gun fire and they had to withdraw. Mr Hollis was completely surrounded by the enemy.

All three guns were destroyed and Hollis, with a few survivors, managed to escape north, spending two days escaping through enemy lines to reach Dunkerque, a feat which earned him a mention in dispatches. He would later go on to win the Military Cross.

The Last Stand at Bambecque

At Bambecque it was reported that enemy infantry were working around the left flank of B Company at 5.00pm, most likely trying to cut the road to Oost-Cappel, while some twenty-five minutes later Grahame Macdonald reported that C Company was being hit by heavy mortar fire and enemy infantry were only about 200 yards from his right flank. With the news that enemy tanks had broken into the village from the east it was decided to strengthen the defences at Battalion Headquarters with the survivors of A and D Companies, utilizing the farm across the road. But it was a nasty road to cross, for the enemy was sweeping it with tracer:

> The men, who were very tired, hesitated, but the Colonel and Jonah stood in the road as calmly as two traffic policemen and their example encouraged the men to cross. As it happened nobody was hit. Evidently the enemy could not see us; the bullets went a little high ... for my part, I kept wondering why the Boche bothered to attack us at all. We could not guard all the roads, and it would have been simple to by-pass us and put us 'in the bag' later.

Haywood's thought on their situation was a little different to that of Private Bailey, who was serving with the Signals Platoon. His recollections are a little more dramatic:

> Enemy shell began to land near the Battalion Headquarters and overhead was the never ending roar of German bombers. The men at Battalion Headquarters were now the only ones to hold back the Germans, the trenches in the orchard were manned, the cooks helping to line the hedges. Machine-gun and rifle fire was on three sides. About a hundred men were now holding that road and it was just a matter of waiting for the assault.

Then, rather miraculously as Haywood described it, Captain Arthur Steele, a liaison officer from the 48th Division, arrived in his car with orders for the battalion to retire. With German tanks now in the rear of the farm, Haywood began preparing maps for B and C Companies to follow to Rexpoëde but the firing from the direction of Bambecque indicated the two companies, although fighting hard, were unlikely to join them.

Little has been written about the last stand of B and C Companies at Bambecque. We do know that two officers from C Company, Lieutenant Roger Cleverley, commanding 14 Platoon, and Lieutenant John Nicolls, commanding 15 Platoon, were taken prisoner. Nicholls' position was overrun and Cleverley was shot in the back and leg and captured the next day, after which he was carried to a German field dressing station. He describes his platoon's position in his diary:

> I and my platoon dug in in an orchard belonging to a farmhouse in the front part of the village to await further orders ... Dusk was falling,

so I posted sentries at strategic points for the night and went down into the village with my batman and an NCO, where we found some bottles of beer, bread and biscuits and tins of sardines. We took back some of these supplies and distributed them as far as possible because, by now, our cookhouse was non-existent.

Cleverley also mentions that Brigade and Battalion Headquarters had 'upsticks and left without informing us of their intentions'. This may refer to the move of Battalion Headquarters to the farm on the Bambecque to Rexpoëde road but, as Haywood says in his account, Johnstone later went down to the village to visit B and C Companies. The attack by the LSAH and tanks of the 2nd Panzer Division was relatively short and completely overwhelmed the Worcesters. Cleverley was wounded:

> Mac (Captain Macdonald) had just left me to visit the other platoons when two tanks appeared at the top of the driveway and opened fire with their 2-pounder guns; then infantry advanced under the cover of their tanks. We fired with our small arms but, of course, we had no weapons to stop the tanks. I received a bullet through my leg and fell into a trench. One of my platoon next to me was hit in the stomach and he fell across my legs, I saw now their tanks had increased to six, so apart from being outnumbered we had run out of ammo . . . I lay in the dugout throughout the night, unable to move because of the other wounded or dead bodies and when things had quietened down and infantry and tanks gone, a small dog crept into the trench and stayed with me the whole of the night. Luckily I survived with a bullet in my lower back near my spine and another in my leg.

Lieutenant Roger Cleverley.

Lieutenant John Nicholls.

The wound Cleverley received in the back was from a pistol fired by, he maintains, the commander of the SS troops. Although he is incorrect with regard to the German unit, who he describes as the SS-*Totenkopf*, it would appear that the murders continued as the *Liebstandarte* moved north:

> The German unit that attacked us was the Waffen-SS, commanded by Capitan (*sic*) W. Mohnke; their policy was that they did not take prisoners, so their commander and another went around the area and shot all the wounded, including myself, with his revolver.

The next day Cleverley was taken to Camiers (near Le Touquet) by Wehrmacht troops, where a field hospital had been setup in a children's home. He says he was in a bed next to a 'man named Norris from the Gloucesters', who was probably Lieutenant Donald Norris. He finally ended up at Laufen but was later moved to other camps, including a period in Colditz. Cleverley was born in 1916 in Bedworth, Warwickshire, educated at King's School, Worcester, and was commissioned in 1938.

Another C Company soldier, Corporal Gilbert Wheeler, was also taken prisoner and confirmed the attacking force were soldiers of the SS:

> My platoon had taken cover in a wheat field, hoping to hide from the Germans. This was ineffective and we were discovered. We were lined up and faced with a row of German soldiers, on motorbikes, all pointing guns at us. We all thought we were going to be shot. The soldier in charge was an SS officer in a very smart uniform, he spoke English.

Helmut Hornbage was part of a German mortar crew and under the orders of *Unterscharführer* Timm of 2 Platoon, 2/Battalion LSAH. He writes of

C Company men at the annual camp at Porthcawl in 1938. Corporal Gilbert Wheeler is kneeling on the left.

the bridge over the Yser at Bambecque being mined and part of his company ending up in the water. This is the first indication that B Company had prepared the bridge for demolition and corroborates Wheeler's and Cleverley's evidence that the Worcesters were attacked by the LSAH.

B Company, which had been widely deployed, fought on until its ammunition was exhausted and then, with the net drawn tightly around it, had no alternative but to surrender. The company commander, Major Frank Ramsey, was taken prisoner along with the survivors of his company. 28-year-old Captain Macdonald, commanding C Company, was killed by mortar fire, but there was no trace of his body when they looked for him. His name is commemorated on the Dunkirk Memorial.

Withdrawal

At 9.00pm Battalion Headquarters withdrew from the farm on the D79 and, with the ever faithful Ted Berry's group acting as rearguard, they left. Berry's well deserved Military Cross was announced in August 1940. Haywood was at the head of the first group to leave:

> I was responsible for finding the way and keeping a sharp lookout for the enemy. I wore my best service-dress, web anklets, a heavy pack and my respirator at the alert. In my left hand I carried the battalion war diary, so I could get rid of it quickly if we ran into trouble. In my right hand I carried my pistol. Behind me came Kenneth Hougham (battalion intelligence officer), then the Colonel and Jonah.

It was understood that Rexpoëde would be held by British troops but as they entered the village there were no signs of any British soldiers. The men of 127 Brigade had been quickly dispatched to defend Rexpoëde and

The Worcesters' Carrier Platoon. Ted Berry is seated in the centre.

The Worcesters were overwhelmed by the *Liebstandarte* Regiment.

Oost-Cappel with the aid of what spare troops and guns could be gathered together. Ammunition was limited to fifty rounds per rifle and 250 rounds per Bren gun as the 1/Highland Light Infantry, 4/East Lancs and 5/Manchesters got involved in some bitter hand to hand fighting, with the troops engaging tanks with grenades.

At Oost-Cappel Captain Charles 'Splosh' Jones, the Brigade Major, knocked out one of the German tanks himself by lobbing a grenade into its open hatch. At Rexpoëde the Highland Light Infantry were completely surrounded, not that it prevented Captain Angus Rose knocking out two German tanks with a Boys rifle. The battalion lost approximately twenty-five killed or wounded. For one officer, 46-year-old Major Henry Adams, it would be a repeat of his experience in 1917, when he was taken prisoner by the Germans; he spent the remainder of the war in Oflag IX.

The order to withdraw was finally received from Brigadier 'Jackie' Smyth after Lieutenant Phillip Kinderley, the Battalion Intelligence Officer, succeeded in getting through to Divisional Headquarters. Unfortunately, by the time the Worcesters crept into Rexpoede, it would appear that the Highlanders had withdrawn.

When the Worcesters arrived nearly every house and shop had been damaged or was on fire. On the pavement lay heaps of broken glass, furniture and rubble. It appeared that they were well and truly surrounded and, as if to add to their predicament, a few yards further on two German tanks were passing over the crossroads from left to right. Johnstone's plan for dealing with them was simple: if they were seen, the anti-tank rifle was to be used to create a diversion, while the remainder of the group attempted to get past using another route. The only downside, as far as Haywood was concerned, was that he was detailed to create the diversion! After an exciting few minutes stalking the tank it became obvious that they were in the clear and the party moved on towards Killem, where they were challenged by 'an unmistakable English voice'. They had reached the comparative safety of Brigade Headquarters.

Chapter 8

Vyfweg and West-Cappel

28–30 May

On 28 May Brigadier Charles Norman and the 1/F&F Yeomanry, under Lieutenant Colonel Ronald Sharp, were ordered to travel north from their positions at Cassel to Vyfweg, where enemy tanks were reported to be menacing the western flank of the Dunkerque Corridor. Brigadier Norman was at Cassel when the orders were received:

> At about the same time the Welsh Guards received orders from III Corps to go to the same area to 'clear up the situation'. I contacted Colonel Copeland-Griffiths, who agreed to move under my command. As 5/RHA in the area could no longer be protected by the reduced Cassel garrison, their CO also agreed to move under me. I agreed to leave the East Riding Yeomanry at Cassel because 145 Brigade could no longer hold their perimeter without their help.

The move of Normans's composite brigade to the north was fraught with difficulties, particularly as the Germans were now apparently across the main Cassel to Bergues road, forcing the convoy to move along minor roads to the east, roads that were jammed with refugee traffic and horsed French artillery units without their guns. Norman was well aware of the disaster that would descend on them if the column was attacked while on the move. As it was, a journey of 15 miles took five hours to complete. It was dark on 28 May by the time Norman met his commanding officers at Vyfweg (Les Cinq Chemins on modern maps), where he explained that the brigade was to defend a 5-mile sector between Bergues and West-Cappel.

6/Green Howards

Arriving some time before Norman was the 6/Green Howards, a 23rd Division unit that had been controlling traffic on the Bergues to Wormhout road the day before. Norman's initial meeting with Lieutenant Colonel Matthew Steel, commanding the Green Howards, was not one that filled him with confidence. Steel explained his battalion was basically a labour battalion of 20-year-old boys:

> They were sent out to France to dig trenches and are only armed with rifles. They have been put into an unsuccessful counter-attack near Gravelines in which they lost heavily – they have been down to the beaches and told they were going home. They were then brought back

and put on the ground where they are now. They will stay so long as they do not see a German. At first sight of the enemy they will bolt to a man.

Norman Deploys his Brigade

Giving Lieutenant Colonel Felix Copeland-Griffiths the freedom to deploy his battalion as he saw fit, Norman established his Brigade Headquarters in a deep ditch about half a mile from the Vyfweg crossroads, along Rue Schoone Straete.

Lieutenant Colonel Gerald Templar, the CO of 5/RHA, suggested that his guns were best placed behind the Canal de Basse Colme. However, rather fortuitously as it turned out, Norman insisted he positioned two sections of guns forward of the canal, ready to fire with open sights at any enemy armoured incursion. Copeland-Griffiths deployed the Prince of Wales Company, under Captain Sir William Makins, to Quaëdypre as an advanced guard, along with a squadron of F&F Yeomanry, until Vyfweg and West-Cappel could be occupied.

When the dust had settled and the Guards were in their allotted positions, they held a rough triangle, of which the base, Vyfweg to West-Cappel, faced south west towards the enemy in Socx, with the apex to the north, at Ratte Ko (La Forge du Rattekoot on modern maps).

The Welsh Guards' Battalion Headquarters was opened at Vyfweg at a farm near to Norman's ditch on Rue Schoone Straete. After withdrawing from Quaëdypre, the triangle was later extended, with Lieutenant John Miller's platoon to include Hoymille and with the Welsh Guards' Prince of Wales Company sharing the 'factory' at the Vyfweg crossroads with B Squadron, 1/F&F Yeomanry. The gaps in the defensive line were filled with the F&F Yeomanry and the Welsh Guards of No. 3 Company, who found themselves in isolated farms, with orders to hang on as long as possible before retiring. Even with the 8/Worcesters at Bambecque, there was still a gap between them and West-Cappel that made the whole defence a rather tenuous affair.

Vyfweg

It was possible that the attacking enemy included the *Großdeutschland* Regiment, although evidence points towards the 20th Motorised Division and the armoured vehicles of the 2nd Panzer Regiment, attacking the Vyfweg crossroads at 7.00am on 29 May.

The first indication that Norman had of the attack was when a crowd of Green Howards came running past his position. In all fairness, the Green Howards' historian (William Synge) does not mention this in his account of the battle, commenting only that, since their successful resistance at Gravelines, the morale of the troops had risen considerably. However, he does mention A Company, on the right of the line, receiving a message to withdraw: 'as it passed Battalion Headquarters, it transpired that the

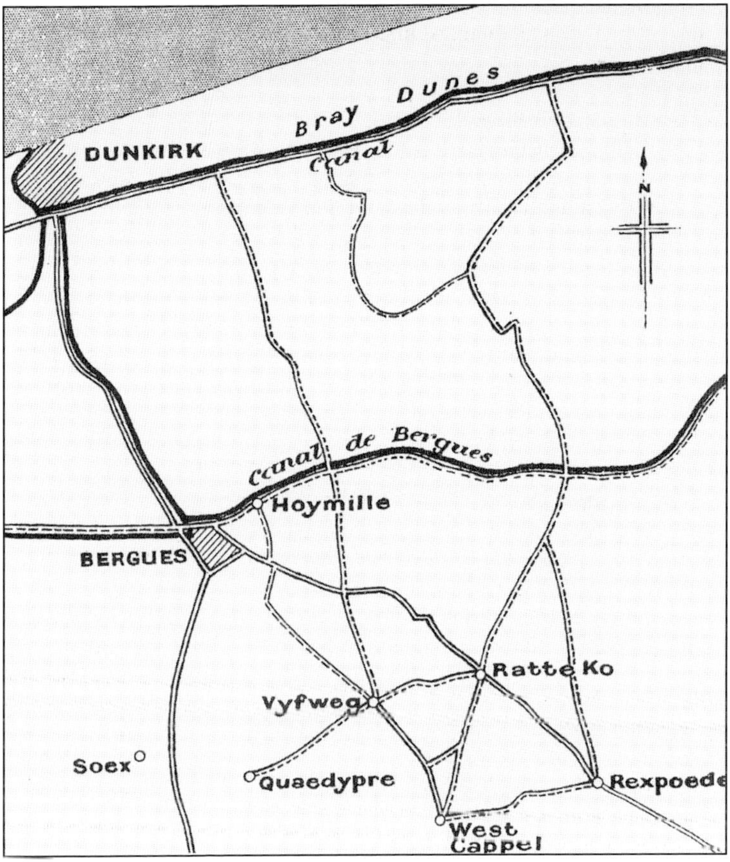

A map of the northern aspect of the battle area, showing West-Cappel in the south and Hoymille in the north.

message had been a mistake and it was ordered back'. Was this the crowd of Green Howards that came running past Norman? Whatever the circumstances, it does seem Norman's account was a little unfair and in any case was probably only representative of one company of Green Howards:

> One of their CSMs and I did our best to rally them and get them into neighbouring ditches – then came the German tanks that had driven them in. I and Major Murray Prain, 1st Fife and Forfar Yeomanry, who was with me, got into a friendly deep ditch which had water in the bottom. As the tanks approached, firing their machine guns, we watched them under our tin hats over the edge of our ditch firing at them with a Boys rifle. The bullets bounced off their front plates like peas. When they got to within 30 or 40 yards they could not depress

their guns enough to hit us. We went to the bottom of the ditch and lay flat on our fronts, wondering what it would be like to have bullets going into my behind and coming out of my mouth.

Fortunately, it was an experience Norman avoided as at that moment the guns of 5/RHA opened up and the enemy were forced to retreat.

In his account of the battle, Captain Jimmy Haggas, commanding B Squadron of the F&F Yeomanry, tells us the crossroads at Vyfweg were under sniper fire from early on 29 May from the two woods west of the crossroads. At about 5.30pm the intensity increased as the enemy began shelling the 'factory' and crossroads. At 6.00pm that evening Major General Thorne arrived for a roadside conference with Norman, at which time it is likely plans for the Brigade's withdrawal were discussed. The F&F Yeomanry war diary gives a flavour of the fighting which took place after Thorne had left:

> The enemy attacked with tanks, coming right through the Welsh Guards and up to our defended ridge, driven back by the forward guns of 5/RHA at Ratte Ko. After the attack was driven off, Brigade, F&F and Welsh Guards, less one forward company still holding its position (at West-Cappel), reformed at Ratte Ko.

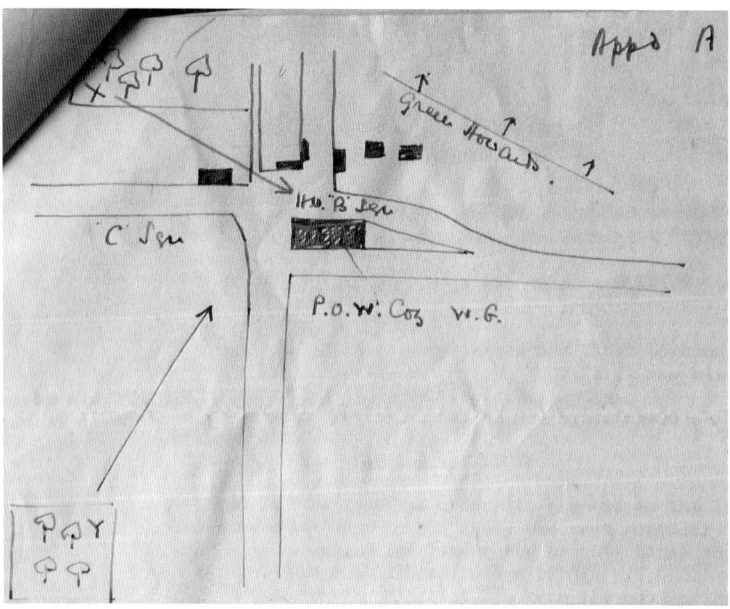

A map taken from the 1/F&F Yeomanry War Diary, showing the crossroads at Vyfweg and the deployment of B and C Squadrons and the Welsh Guards' Prince of Wales Company. German snipers were operating from the two copses on the left.

Firing under open sights, the two forward sections of RHA guns were certainly proving their worth. While this was going on around them, Captain Haggas was asked by Copeland-Griffiths to take his Adjutant, Captain Archie Noel, to Brigade Headquarters for further orders:

> On our way we were fired upon by machine guns and I think some heavier stuff. I found Brigadier Norman with Lieutenant Colonel Sharp under heavy machine-gun fire. They were standing in a shallow pit. The Brigadier gave us orders to take back to Copeland-Griffiths, instructing him to withdraw the Welsh Guards.

Haggas and Archie Noel had been fired upon from west of the Guards' Battalion Headquarters, which did little damage to his light tank but, minutes after he left Norman's ditch, Sharp and Captain Forster Jennings, the F&F Medical Officer, were killed by a shell.

Captain Otho Bullivant, the F&F Adjutant, thinks orders for the withdrawal were passed on to Norman's units around 7.00pm; most managed to get to the coast but those unlucky men in the Guards' Headquarters building were rushed by German infantry, capturing, amongst others, Archie Noel and RSM Richards. Norman was one of the lucky ones who evaded capture; he retired from the army as a major general in 1946.

West-Cappel

The greatest weight of the German attack appeared to have fallen on West-Cappel. For the officers and men of the Welsh Guards who had been deployed there by Copeland-Griffiths, it is not even known if the orders for withdrawal even reached them.

Men of the 1/F&F Yeomanry outside Buckingham Palace after receiving their medals. *Left to right*: Trooper Leslie Gill MM, Corporal Arthur Allen MM, TSM John Stewart DCM, TSM Percy Brown DCM and Sergeant William Anderson MM.

Captain Jocelyn Gurney and the Welsh Guards' Number 2 Company had arrived in the early morning of 29 May. Keeping his headquarters with the RASC drivers and their vehicles in the grounds behind the fourteenth century Château Briarde, he positioned PSM Hubert Maisey with 6 Platoon to cover the northern approaches and 19-year-old Second Lieutenant Rhidian Llewellyn with 5 Platoon to cover the south eastern roads towards Wylder and Bambecque. This left Second Lieutenant Nick Daniel and 4 Platoon to dig in around the church. The first sign of enemy activity came just after midday, when 5 Platoon reported a German patrol on their front. It was not until 3.00pm that Llewellyn reported that a strong force of tanks and infantry were advancing form Wylder and was concerned that they might be overrun; Gurney sent a runner and ordered 5 Platoon to return to the château.

From Llewellyn's account it appears that the withdrawal was going relatively smoothly until his last section was about to leave:

> The section was shot up as they went down the road . . . I raced back to the last Bren gunner, Guardsman Warwick, who was firing in bursts to his front. Our time to leave had come but which way to go? I knew our retreat had now been cut off and as Warwick had been firing for some time I found it difficult to get him out of his slit trench, he was very stiff. I picked up his Bren gun for him . . . I put the gun into the hip firing position and Warwick was close at hand with loaded magazines. We worked our way down the hedge towards the church and the

Château Briarde, showing the bridge that possibly sheltered both Gurney and Llewellyn from German tanks.

> 4 Platoon positions. When Warwick and I came out of the church gateway, the lane was full of Germans. I fired several bursts at them and sent them scampering down the lane. I fired after them and used up a full magazine. We ran into more Germans at the rear of the houses, some were firing at us and one of two put their hands up. We ran through them and I kept firing all the time.

Llewellyn and Warwick made it back to 4 Platoon's positions, where there was a short conversation with Nick Daniel, who by this time was coming under considerable pressure himself – presumably from the same Germans that Llewellyn had just dispersed with his Bren gun. After making his way back to the rear of the château to report, Gurney decided to assess the situation facing 4 Platoon and Daniel for himself:

> I crawled away towards the moat and I was in the ditch when two tanks came into the garden and shot at me. I dived under the moat bridge and there I was, with a tank pounding at the bridge above me. Luckily he didn't see the moat, went into it and stuck; but his gun was trained on the château door. Eventually my servant crawled out to me and I decided we must make for the château. As we got out of the moat, Daniel and some of 4 Platoon came in. They had one man on a stretcher and I said we must make a dash for it and picked up the front end of the stretcher. Guardsman (Ivor) Llewellyn had the other end. As we made for the door of the château, the tank in the moat fired and caught Llewellyn and killed him.

Daniel had been lucky to get away with a few survivors and had no idea that PSM Maisey and 6 Platoon had already been overwhelmed in the north of the village. At the same time as Gurney and his party were making a break for the chateau door, another tank moved in on the battalion transport and company headquarters. Rhidian Llewellyn and Guardsman Andrews narrowly avoided being shot up by the tank:

> We were the last to leave company headquarters and we worked our way back to the château but reached the bridge over the moat at the same time as the tank, fire from which wounded me in the right hand. Andrews and I dived under the bridge from where Captain Gurney and party had just made it to the chateau door some minutes before.

Recent research has suggested that it was not the bridge across the moat at the front of the chateau but that at its rear. Whichever door was used, they remained where they were for the next two hours while the battle raged on above them, both men wondering if the enemy would eventually discover them. At 7.30pm a lull in the fighting allowed Llewellyn and Andrews to creep out of the moat and enter the château by a side entrance:

> Inside the château we now had about thirty-five of our people, these included Captain Gurney, Nick Daniels and a few of 4 Platoon,

A photograph of the rear of the Château Briarde that later research has suggested was the entrance that Llewellyn used after sheltering in the moat.

> Guardsman Savage, a stretcher bearer who did magnificent work throughout the battle, PSM Christian and most of my platoon … The company had already lost about a hundred men … by 9.00pm Captain Gurney thought the Germans were about to renew the attack on the château so, while he and PSM Christian covered our withdrawal, we crawled down the steps … Private (Austin) Snead reported the Germans were creeping closer and they opened fire. We fled, crossing the road under fire and met up near the 6 Platoon position from where German voices were heard.'

Escape

Surrounded and cut off by German infantry and tanks, they managed to find a gap and at 10.00pm they began an epic night march across country. Having to fight on at least two occasions as they passed through German lines, they arrived at the Canal de Basse Colme at 3.00am on 30 May. As the crow flies, West-Cappel to Bray Dunes is a little over 10 miles and their escape and subsequent march was a journey that must place Gurney's men amongst the breakouts made by the 2/Dorsets at Festubert and the 5/Gloucesters at Ledringhem. Llewellyn's last words on the West-Cappel episode simply stated that they reported to Copeland-Griffiths on the beach at Bray Dunes and the battalion sailed for England at 10.00pm that night. What he fails to say is that only three officers and twenty-one other ranks reached Bray Dunes! Llewellyn's award of the Military Cross was published along with that of Jocelyn Gurney in October 1940.

Gurney died in Norfolk in 1973 and Nick Daniel in 1994; Rhidian Llewellyn survived them both, passing away in 2008, aged eighty-eight.

Chapter 9

The Tours

General Advice to tourers

Although there are several opportunities for the battlefield visitor to stretch their legs during the tour, there are also short walks, one in Ledringhem and the other in Les Cinq Chemins. A further walk/drive is in Wormhout. The author strongly suggests obtaining maps from the various Tourist Offices along the route to supplement your excursions and taking time to prepare at home before you arrive. While much of the area covered by the guide is dotted with cafés and other refreshment venues, it is always wise to have something to eat and drink with you.

Maps

The tours described in this book are best supported by the IGN *Série Bleu* 1:25000 maps, which can be purchased at most good tourist offices, the bigger local supermarkets and online from www.mapsworldwide.com. The area of Wormhout, Ledringhem and points north as described in the text, are all contained within the Carte de Randonnée 2303E Wormhout and Cassel and 2403O Steenvoorde. Visitors may also find Carte de Randonnée 2302O Dunkerque useful. Bear in mind that satellite navigation can be a very useful supplement in supporting general route finding, particularly when trying to locate obscure CWGC cemeteries; and it is always useful to use the street view on Google Earth prior to any visit.

Travel and Where to Stay

By far the quickest passage across the Channel is via the Tunnel at Folkstone, the thirty-six minutes travelling time comparing favourably with the longer ferry journey from Dover to Calais or Dunkerque. Whether your choice of route is over or under the Channel, early booking is always recommended if advantage is to be taken of the cheaper fares. Travelling times vary according to traffic; but as a rough guide the journey from Calais to Wormhout is 35 miles via the A16, a drive of about fifty minutes.

With regard to accommodation, you have the choice of staying locally in Wormhout or Cassel or on the coast at Dunkerque. Wormhout lacks some of the more well known chain hotels but there is plenty of good self catering and B&B accommodation in the area.

There is much more choice at **Cassel** and the author can recommend the four-star **Hotel Chatellerie de Schoebeque**, offering good quality accommodation, a spa, free WiFi and parking and an excellent restaurant. The two-star **Hotel Restaurant de Foch** offers a good restaurant and comfortable rooms. If you are intending to base yourself in or around **Dunkerque** the author can recommend the three-Star **Hôtel Welcome**, which is located in the centre of Dunkerque. It offers 24-hour reception and en-suite accommodation with free Wi-Fi access. Alternatively, the three-Star **All Suites Appart Hôtel** is said to be of a good standard and is situated on the waterfront – only a short walk from the Bastion 32 Museum. There are numerous apartments in both Dunkerque and the neighbouring towns of Malo-lés-Bains and Bray-Dunes, details of which can be found on the internet. Visitors should book early to avoid disappointment. As with other areas, the region abounds with B&B accommodation that can be found on the internet.

For those who prefer the outdoor life, **Camping des Roses** at Esquelbecq is a 3-Star, clean site with a restaurant, bar and WiFi. **Camping Municipal la Licorne** has the convenience of being near the beach at Dunkerque and, apart from having several plots for motor homes, also boasts thirty-four holiday homes. A little further south is **Camping Château du Gandspette** at Éperlecques, a campsite which is amongst the author's favourites. Situated some eighteen minutes from Wormhout, the site offers a swimming pool, a restaurant and Wi-Fi and a number of mobile homes for rent. Further information on all aspects of accommodation can be obtained from the various Tourist Offices in the main centres at Dunkerque, Malo-lés-Bains, Bray-Dunes and De Panne.

Driving

Driving abroad is not the expedition it was years ago and most battlefield visitors may well have already made the journey several times. However, if this is the first time you have ventured on French roads there are one or two common sense rules to take into consideration. Ensure your vehicle is properly insured and covered by suitable breakdown insurance; if in doubt contact your insurer, who will advise you. There are also a number of compulsory items to be carried by motorists that are required by French law. These include your driving licence and vehicle registration documents, a warning triangle, a *Conformité Européenne* (CE) approved fluorescent safety vest for each person travelling in the car, headlamp beam convertors and the visible display of a UK plate. Even if not a requirement by now, it is advisable to have a green card for your insurance.

Whereas some modern cars have built in headlamp convertors and many have a UK plate incorporated into the rear number plate, French law also requires the vehicle to be equipped with a first aid kit and, if not now, sooner or later a a breath test kit. If you fail to have these available there are some hefty on the spot fines for these motoring offences if caught driving without them. Most, if not all, of these items can be purchased at the various outlets at the Tunnel, the Channel port at Dover and on board the ferries themselves. On a more personal note it is always advisable to take out personal accident insurance and a reserve supply of any medication that you may be taking at the time may also be useful.

Here are three tips that the author has always found useful:

1. When driving on single carriageway roads try to stop at petrol stations on the right hand side of the road. It is much more natural then to continue driving on the right hand side of the road after you leave. Leaving a garage or supermarket is often the time when you find yourself naturally turning onto the wrong side of the road. Garages are often unmanned and require you to pay at the pump with your credit card – so be warned when you fill up.
2. Take your time! Don't rush! If you rush your instinct may take over and your instinct is geared to driving on the left and remember, indicators are often not used and the direction some vehicles are intending to take can be difficult to determine.
3. Pay particular care on roundabouts. A lot of drivers do not or rarely appear to use indicators. Navigators, remember to look at the signs anti-clockwise and drivers remember that the danger is coming from the left.

Visiting Commonwealth War Graves Commission Cemeteries

The CWGC cemeteries visited in this guide are often to be found in communal cemeteries, such as **Wormhoudt Communal Cemetery**, although you will find British casualties from 1940 located in a number of existing First World War Cemeteries, such as **Croix Rouge Military Cemetery** and **Arneke British Cemetery**.

Visitors should also remember that where a soldier has been recovered from the battlefield it was not always possible to identify exactly when he was killed or died. To that end, on some headstones the CWGC has provided two dates, between which, it is presumed, the individual died. When visiting the fallen from the Second World War in the area, it is impossible not to be reminded constantly of casualties from the First World War, the numbers of which probably horrified the men of the BEF who fought in this area during May 1940.

The visitor will also come across the graves of aircrew that were shot down over the course of the war and those men who died during the 1944 advance after the D-Day landings. The graves of men killed in the area during May and June 1940 are probably some of the least visited in the whole of Northern France. The small numbers of men, whose headstones are sometimes lost amongst the myriad of French civilian graves in communal cemeteries, are often all but forgotten.

The Imperial (since the early 1960s the Commonwealth), War Graves Commission, was responsible for introducing the standardized headstone, which brought equality in death regardless of rank, race or creed, and it is this familiar white headstone that you will see now in CWGC cemeteries all

over the world. Cemeteries are usually well signposted and visitors should keep an eye open for the green and white directional signs. Where there is a CWGC plot within a communal or churchyard cemetery, the familiar green and white sign at the entrance with the words *Tombes de Guerre du Commonwealth* will indicate their presence. French military cemeteries are usually marked by the French national flag, whilst those which are contained within communal cemeteries are often marked by a sign at the cemetery entrance bearing the words: *Carre Militaire, Tombes de Soldats, Morts pour la France.*

Route 1: Ledringhem

Start and finish: *Mairie* at Ledringhem
Distance: 1.5 miles
Suitable for: 🚶 🚲

There is very little to see in Arnèke and, unless you wish to visit the site of the Gloucesters brief stay in the village and the cemetery, your time may well be better spent at Ledringhem. **Arneke British Cemetery** contains 435 First World War burials and five from the Second World War, of which three are identified. The graves are mainly 1918 vintage.

This short walk covers the *Mairie* at Ledringhem and the route of the Gloucester' breakout and successful evacuation. Park in the obvious car park near the church (the observant amongst you will notice the car charging points located in the corner of the car park). From the car park the ***Mairie*** is immediately on your left, as is the churchyard where Major Waller was killed. The church tower is where the Forward Operating Officer from 24/Field Regiment was posted.

Pass the *Mairie* and walk down the path until the road is reached.

Turn right along the D55 Route de Wormhout and continue past two roads on the right to reach Chemin d'Heenhout. Turn right here and walk along the road until you come to a private house with a windmill motif on the exterior wall. Walk to the next bend and stop. The **Guillemin Windmill** was probably in the fields to your left and the orchard was where the modern housing estate is now on the opposite side of the road. On your

The *Mairie* at Ledringhem.

The cemetery and churchyard at Ledringhem.

The Church at Ledringhem, with its tower just visible.

Chemin d'Heenhout.

return visit the **Ledringhem Churchyard Cemetery** which has forty-four burials, all of the Second World War, including **Lieutenant Basil Glasspool** of the Cheshires and **Major Anthony Waller** of the Gloucesters. There are twenty-four casualties from the 5/ Gloucesters, the remainder being from the Cheshires, Warwickshires and Royal Artillery.

Ledringhem Churchyard Cemetery.

Route 2: Les Cinq Chemins, Quaëdypre

Start and finish: Pont a Poissons, Les Cinq Chemins, by the former Prince of Wales Company Headquarters.
Distance: 1.5 miles
Suitable for: 🚶 🚲

This is another short walk, taking in the Prince of Wales Company Headquarters, B Squadron of the Fife and Forfar and the Battalion Headquarters of the 1/Welsh Guards. We move on to discover the location of Brigadier Charles Norman's ditch, where he took shelter with Major Murray Prain.

The Welsh Guards were part of Brigadier Norman's mobile brigade and were transferred from Cassel to another threatened flank position south of Bergues at Vyfweg and West-Cappel. This walk is focused on the road leading from Les Cinq Chemins to Norman's ditch. Number 2 Company were at West Cappel and bore the brunt of the infantry of the German attack while another Welsh Guards strongpoint was at Ratte Ko (La Forge du Rattekoott). This was the so-called Triangle of Defence.

From your vehicle, which is parked outside the large building that formally housed the Prince of Wales Company, cross the road onto Rue Schoone Straete and walk down the road to the first farm on the right. This was the battalion headquarters of the Welsh Guards, from where Lieutenant Colonel Copeland-Griffiths commanded his much dispersed battalion and here would have been Headquarters Company. The farm is

The farm driveway leading to the Welsh Guards' Battalion Headquarters.

private property and should not be approached. Return to the roadway and continue to the next farm on the right. A walk up to the farm will reveal the remnants of a ditch across to the left and this is probably where Brigadier Norman took shelter with Major Prain.

Return to the road and on your way back to the vehicle you should get an excellent view of the Welsh Guards' Prince of Wales Company Headquarters, commanded by Captain Sir William Makins. The building with the white windows to the left of the Prince of Wales Company Headquarters was originally a single story house but after the war an upper floor was added.

With the Germans pressing hard, Lieutenant Colonel Sharp, commanding the Fife and Forfar Yeomanry and Captain Foster Jennings the battalion medical officer, were killed by a shell that landed on the battalion headquarters. They are buried in Wareham Communal Cemetery. The battalion headquarters was eventually rushed by German infantry, with most of the men getting away with the exception of RSM Richards and Captain Archie Noel, the Welsh Guards' adjutant, who were taken prisoner. Norman escaped to become commander of 27 Armoured Brigade

Cemeteries

Rexpöde Communal Cemetery There are twenty-two Second World War casualties commemorated in this site. Of these, eleven are unidentified. Two second lieutenants of the 1/Highland Light Infantry were killed on

Norman's ditch is on the left of the photograph, possibly near to the hedge.

The Welsh Guards' Prince of Wales Company HQ still dominates Rue Schoone Straete.

29 May: **John Ker Cross** (A9) and **Kenneth Norman-Wright** (A.7). They are buried with five others from the same regiment.

Croix Rouge Military Cemetery, Quaëdypre There are two identified casualties of the Second World War and one unknown amongst ninety First World War graves. They are **Lance Corporal Eric Smith**, killed/died on 22 May, of 248/Field Company and **Private Arthur Freer** of 13/Field Ambulance, killed/died on 28 May.

West-Cappel Churchyard Of the thirty-eight casualties, twenty are members of the 1/Welsh Guards, the remainder include eight men of the 8/ Worcestershire Regiment.

The entrance gates of Rexpode Communal Cemetery, with the distinctive CWGC plaque on the right pillar.

West-Cappel Churchyard Cemetery.

Route 3: The Massacre of the Innocents

Start and finish: The former Estaminet St Hubert, Place du Général de Gaulle, Wormhout.
Distance: 4 miles
Suitable for: 🚶 🚲 🚗

Start at the former Estaminet St Hubert (the new café is across the street near to the church). The former café is still distinctive and was where the SS men retired prior to marching the prisoners to the Plaine au Bois. For those of you who are completing the route by car, it would be an idea **to park your vehicle somewhere on the Route de Ledringhem** after you have walked along Rue de l'Église, thus enabling you to drive from there to Rue de Rubrouck towards Ferme de Fort Rosé.

Walk along **Rue de l'Église to the house at the end, Number 26**. It was outside this house that Gunner Richard Parry estimates that the prisoners were compelled to hold up their arms for at least a quarter of an hour until a German appeared from the Estaminet St Hubert and gave permission for the prisoners to rest their arms.

Moving through the town the prisoners turned left after Rue de I'Ëglise and then probably right into Rue de Rubrouck, past the parkland on the right. After 50 yards there is now a roundabout on Rue de Rubrouck and the road continues out of town past the sports complex until **Ferme de Fort Rosé** is reached on the left of the road and where there is an information board. The Ferme had originally been the headquarters of A Company,

The former Café Hubert is almost opposite the church.

Number 26, Rue de L'Église.

Ferme de Fort Rosé.

2/Warwicks, under Major Cecil Chichester-Constable and it was not until many years later that a number of British items were discovered hidden in the roof of one of the stables. They are now in the museum at Llandudno.

Following the demise of A Company, 2/Warwicks, the Ferme became the Battalion Headquarters of the *Liebstandarte*'s 2/Battalion and the prisoners were halted outside, the SS Guards presumably waiting for instructions for the disposal of the captives. According to Leslie Aitken's book, *Massacre on the Road to Dunkirk*, at this point a senior SS Officer came out of the building and 'was raving blue murder.' One of the prisoners who understood German then exclaimed: 'My god! They're taking no prisoners'.

As the prisoners were herded across a nearby field they were subjected to a torrent of abuse and those who were unable to keep up were either shot, bayoneted or kicked. As the party neared its destination it became apparent that it was not the farm, which they could see immediately ahead, but a small barn near a row of trees. The men were ordered inside the barn, which was surrounded by twelve SS guards.

Continue past the Ferme de Fort Rosé and take the first road on the right, Rue des Dunkirk Veterans. This road will take you in 300 yards to the entrance to the **Plaine au Bois**. 170 yards along this track is the reconstructed barn, which was erected in 2000, along with the lookout and an orientation table. There are numerous information boards around the field explaining the significance of the features.

The entrance to Plaine au Bois.

The reconstructed barn.

The pond where Captain Lynn-Allen and Gunner Richard Parry were shot.

Esquelbecq Military Cemetery.

Leave the Plaine au Bois and turn right towards Esquelbecq. If you are driving/cycling this is perhaps a good moment to visit **Esquelbecq Military Cemetery**. Those who are walking will possibly wish to visit the cemetery at the completion of the route. The cemetery is west of the village and south of the D17, Zeggers-Cappel road, off the Rue du Souvenir, and contains 578 casualties of the First World War and forty-seven casualties from the Second World War, along with a small number of French and German casualties. It is quite possible that many of the victims of the barn massacre at Wormhout may also be amongst the unidentified burials in Esquelbecq Military Cemetery. Here you will find 36-year-old **WOII Augustus Jennings** (Sp Mem 3F) and 24-year-old **Sergeant Stanley Moore** (Sp Mem 3F), who threw themselves on the first of the grenades that the SS Guards directed into the barn.

Return to the D7, Rue de Wormhout, drive slowly out of Esquelbecq and pass the turning on the left (Rue de Calvaire). In less than half a mile, on the right hand side of the road, is **a memorial remembering the massacre that took place at the barn on 28 May 1940**. This is the same memorial pictured in Chapter 6.

The memorial on the D17.

Continue along the D17 until you see a line of white posts on the left hand side of the road and a private building opposite. The building is called **le Rossignol** and it was approximately here that the roadblock was established and Sepp Dietrich and Max Wünche had to shelter in the drainage ditch from the hail of British machine gun bullets.

Continue into Wormhout and stop just before the junction with Place du Général de Gaulle, where there is parking and two electrical charging stations for vehicles. This is the site of the former Château Morael, which was destroyed in the air raid of 27 May 1940. The château was the headquarters of 2/Royal Warwickshire regiment and 53/Anti-Tank Regiment. An information board contains a picture of the ruined château. Today the site is occupied by a large shop.

Turn right to find Estaminet St Hubert and the interesting church, which is a short walk along the main street.

Cemetery

Wormhoudt Communal Cemetery The cemetery can be found on the east side of the D916 at the crossroads with Rue Roger Denbanck; a narrow road, which is marked *Cimetière* – keep your eyes peeled – leads down to the cemetery. British casualties are mainly of the Second World; there are four identified casualties from 1916.

Gunner Jack Creed of 53/Anti-Tank Regiment was positioned at the crossroads with his gun and he, together with those that escaped, ran

The drainage ditch (on right) where Dietrich and Wünsche had to take shelter; and le Rossignol, where the road block was situated.

The shop that now occupies the ground on which Château Morael once stood.

The entrance to Wormhoudt Communal Cemetery; CWGC burials are at its left rear.

through the cemetery on their way to the 8/Worcestershire Battalion Headquarters. The CWGC casualties can be found straight ahead from the entrance gates. Two names appear on the majority of the headstones in the CWGC plot and it is thought that many of the victims of the barn massacre at Wormhout may well be amongst the myriad of unidentified burials at the cemetery. Buried here are **Major Cecil Chichester-Constable** (A.42) the commander of A Company 2/Royal Warwicks, **Major James Rance** (B.21) who commanded Headquarters Company, 2/Royal Warwicks and 22-year-old **Lieutenant David Padfield** (A.48) of A Company, 2/Royal Warwicks. Others include **Major John Crichton** (F.13), attached to 12/Lancers and **Second Lieutenant Mervyn Edwards** (A.42), 57/Anti-Tank Regiment. Edwards was awarded the Military Cross shortly before his death.

Bibliography

Primary Sources

The National Archives

Unit War Diaries in WO 166 and WO 167

Personal accounts and Diaries in CAB 106 and WO 217

PoW Reports in WO 344 and WO 373

The Imperial War Museum Sound Archive

The Imperial War Museum Department of Documents

The National Army Museum

The Liddell Hart Military Archive, London

The RUSI Library The Worcestershire and Mercian Regimental Museum Archives

Published Sources

Aitkin, L., *Massacre on the Road to Dunkirk*.

Blaxland, G., *Destination Dunkirk: The Story of Gort's Army*, William Kimber, 1973.

Creed, J., *Mars and Venus*, Brewin Books, 2000.

Crook, A., *Barbed-Wire Doctor*, Pentland Press, 1986.

Cuncliffe M., *The History of the Royal Warwickshire Regiment 1919–1995*, William Clowes, 1956.

Ellis, L.F., The *Welsh Guards at War*, London Stamp Exchange, 1989.

Ellis, L.F., *The War in France and Flanders*, HMSO, 1953.

Farndale, M., *History of the Royal Regiment of Artillery*, Brasseys, 1996.

Frieser, K.-H., *The Blitzkrieg Legend*, Naval Institute Press, 2012.

Guderian, H., *Panzer Leader*, Michael Joseph, 1952.

Hart, L., *The Rommel Papers*, Collins, 1953.

Jackson, J., *The Fall of France*, OUP, 2003.

Lynch, T., *Dunkirk 1940, 'Whereabouts Unknown'*, History Press, 2010.

Meyer, K., *Grenadiers*, Stackpole, 2005.

Murland, J., *Retreat and Rearguard: Dunkirk 1940*, Pen & Sword, 2015.

Daniell, D., *Cap of Honour*, Harrap, 1951.

Philson, A., *The British Army 1939–1945 Organization and Order of Battle, Volume 6*, Naval and Military Press, 2007.

Rigby & Ellis, *Ever Glorious, Volume 2*, The Regiment, 2007.

Rommelaere, G., *The Forgotten Massacre*, Warwick Printing Co., 2001.

Sebag-Montefiore, H., *Dunkirk – Fight to the Last Man*, Viking, 2006.

Index